**20 Philosophies To Help You Understand And Control
The Different Ways Stress Attacks Your Life**

# Building Blocks
# For Controlling Stress

*Learning To Make Stress a Friend,
Not An Enemy*

Richard Flint, CSP

**"** There is a dichotomy to stress. Stress can be healthy and it can be life threatening. While each of us experience stress, Richard provides a blueprint for building a life that is stressless. You'll learn 20 key tactics that will empower you to enjoy a healthier and more active lifestyle. **"**
— Lawton W. Howell, Sr., Chief Executive Officer, WellnessOne Corporation

**"** After having read hundreds of self-help, personal development and motivational-inspirational books, it's refreshing to read Richard Flint's <u>Building Blocks for Controlling Stress</u>. Richard teaches common sense solutions based on real-life experiences. As a good teacher, he teaches based on principle and according to a pattern. This is a primer on basic life skills that can change thousands of lives in a positive way. As the day-to-day stresses build in this unsettling time we need all the help and encouragement we can get. Proverbs 12:24-25 says, 'Work hard and become a leader, be lazy and become a slave. Worry weighs a person down; an encouraging word cheers a person up.' NLT **"**
— Ken Dockery, National Field Development Leader for Vollara, Inc.,
The Uncompromising Health Company

**"** Richard offers wise insight into the underlying behavior that allows stress to sabotage our happiness and productivity. Each chapter provides key thoughts and actions that give tools to manage stress and create a calm and productive life. This book is a lifeline in our complex world! **"**
— Lauren Fisher, Top Performing Medicals Sales Professional, KCI Medical

" Who would believe that stress could be both positive and negative?...
...In this book, Richard provides his 20 Philosophies as a benchmark
in which a person can understand and control the different ways that
stress attacks one's life on a daily basis. Richard's philosophies are
not designed to eliminate stress. These philosophies provide us the
ability and insight to gain the pace, calmness, clarity, and confidence
to properly make the decisions and choices when presented with the
"Tests" that life brings at us. In fact, as we control our behavior and
emotions the "Tests" become our friends. That is the beauty of who we
are! The "Tests" are actually the measuring device for us to confirm
that our journey of life is filled with growth and purpose. This is a must
read for everyone. These 20 Philosophies are really a gift to all of us
from Richard... Thank you my friend! "

— **Dr. Ted Gehrig, DDS, Lincoln Park Columbus Dental Associates, Chicago, IL**

Published 2012
Copyright 2012

ISBN# 0-937851-35-3
Flint, Inc. Product #3014

*Printed in the United States of America.*
*For information write to*
*Richard Flint International*
*11835 Canon Blvd., Suite C-105*
*Newport News, VA 23606-2570*
*or call 1-800-368-8255*

*info@richardflint.com*

**www.RichardFlint.com**

Cover Design by Denise Smith

# DEDICATION

*To Steve Sands who, in the midst of all that has been thrown at him, stands tall and hasn't caved into the negative stress that sought to destroy his life.*

# TABLE OF CONTENTS

# BUILDING BLOCKS
## FOR CONTROLLING STRESS

**Building Block #1:**
*People who work to eliminate stress become stressful; people who learn to control their stress enhance their creativity.*

**Building Block #2:**
*Stress is the result of emotions, not the events in your life.*

**Building Block #3:**
*Stress in any one room of your life will find its way into all the rooms of your life.*

**Building Block #4:**
*Negative fear is the root cause of most of your negative stress.*

**Building Block #5:**
*The only definition your life has to truth is what you tell it.*

**Building Block #6:**
*Life is not about asking questions; it is about learning to ask the right questions.*

**Building Block #7:**
*When your mind and your emotions are at war, you will feel it mentally, emotionally, physically and spiritually.*

**Building Block #8:**
*Increase your pace and you increase your stress.*

**Building Block #9:**
*Negative behavior creates negative stress.*

**Building Block #10:**
*Anger takes stress to the danger zone.*

**Building Block #11:**
*Worry, for the most part, is an emotion that creates tension where it is not necessary.*

**Building Block #12:**
*Procrastination is not a behavior that creates freedom; it is a hostage taker.*

**Building Block #13:**
*Disorganized people are stressful to self and others.*

**Building Block #14:**
*If you can't control your personal tiredness, you can't control your stress.*

**Building Block #15:**
*When you don't trust yourself, you will make decisions that will add stress to your life.*

**Building Block #16:**
*Staying in the wrong place makes life very stressful.*

**Building Block #17:**
*Every situation in life provides you with a test. Your behavior determines whether you get through or have to repeat the event.*

**Building Block #18:**
*The lack of a personal dream increases the negative stress in your life.*

**Building Block #19:**
*When life hands you the unexpected, it will increase your personal stress.*

**Building Block #20:**
*No joke! Stress can kill you!*

## LAYING THE FOUNDATION
## FOR THIS BOOK
### *Stress Is a Fact*

Have you ever met a person without stress in their life? I'll bet you haven't! If you are breathing, you have stress. That is a fact.

The question is what aspect of stress you are dealing with. Does it keep you at a manageable pace, or does it send you over the edge? Does it work with you or against you?

What many don't understand is there is good stress and bad stress. Good stress is healthy. It has a positive purpose in your life. Bad stress is dangerous and can mentally, emotionally and physically destroy your life.

Several years ago I wrote my first book on stress, The Truth About Stress, and it had a major impact on the lives of those who read it. Many told me "for the first time I understand what stress is all about."

In writing that book I wrestled with defining the term "stress" at a level the average person could understand. In my research I found 102 different definitions. That made me stressful.

Most who have defined the term have either made it so technical it creates more stress for the person, or they have defined it using results, not understanding. That simply leaves the person confused, and confusion feeds your stress.

The personal definition I came up with was *stress is anything in your life that makes you uptight*. That's a pretty simple definition that contains some pretty in-depth insights.

If you simply look at the concept of "uptight," it takes you to every corner of your life. That means stress can happen just by the alarm clock going off, and you not wanting to get up. It can happen as you try to decide what to wear. It can continue as you make your decision about what to have for breakfast; it can continue with your drive to work; challenges at work can make you uptight -- phone calls, meetings, work to get done, people pulling you in all directions, ending your day with more on your plate than you started with.

Get the picture? Stress is anything that makes you uptight.

That means anything that takes you out of sync creates stress. Now — does that make stress a constant negative? NO! Sometimes being uptight is a good thing. There are times when your life needs to slow down. You get this feeling things are moving too fast, or there are too many things going on in your life. You feel this need to slow down. At this point stress is a good thing. You listen to what you are feeling and make the adjustment in your pace. Achieving this brings your life back in sync, and the result is you feel better.

Now — take this to the other side. You feel your life is moving too fast, or there are too many things going on in your life, BUT you don't listen to what you are feeling. Instead of slowing down and bringing things under control, you either ignore what is happening or you speed up. This also creates stress, BUT the stress here is not good. This is dangerous stress; this is negative stress. What you are doing is putting your mind, your emotions, your physical being on a collision course with each other. The reality is *they will collide and the collision will not be healthy.* The result will be some form of mental, emotional or physical breakdown.

Hey, have you ever had so much pressure on you that you started feeling tired? The more you stared at what was happening the greater the tiredness became. Then, one day you just don't feel well; in fact you are sick. Have you ever been there? That's negative stress at work in your life.

Let me pose some other questions for you:
- *Have you ever been so mentally exhausted you were physically wiped out?*
- *Have you ever been so physically tired that mentally you had a headache?*
- *Have you ever been so emotionally drained that you just couldn't think?*
- *Have you ever had so much going on in your head, you felt your head was going to explode?*
- *Have you ever just been so wiped out you didn't want to do anything?*

Do you understand what is happening to you? Your internal system of checks and balances is working to keep you from going into overload. The three aspects of you—*your mind, your emotions, your physical presence*—work to protect you from destroying yourself. When one aspect is moving toward overload, the other two kick in to take some of the pressure off of you. The challenge is too many don't listen to what they are being told and just move forward with even greater speed. Then, there is the collision and you find yourself out of control. Most will look around and blame the events that led to the collision. The truth is the event had nothing to do with what has happened. The event "was." The collision is the result of feelings demonstrated through behavior.

When you don't listen to what your inside voices are saying, they will force you to listen. What you have done is taken the positive side of stress and turned it into something negative and destructive.

Your life revolves around Events, Feelings and Choices. If you ask the average person which one of these creates stress, the majority would answer "the Events." The truth is *the event is not the point of stress.* The Event simply "is."

Others would tell you that the stress is created when you have to make a choice about what to do with the Event. The truth is the choice is not the stress. It is after the fact. It is the last step in the process.

The stress comes from your feelings. The Event is outside of you. The Choice is the outer demonstration of action. Stress is an emotion that is defined by the feelings you bring to the Event that control the Choice you will make.

When you approach the Event with positive emotions, you are calm with your Choice, and the result is positive stress. Yes, you were uptight. Yes, you may have felt anxious or nervous, BUT you looked at the Event, planned a journey, trusted yourself and moved forward with positive feelings about the outcome. The stress you felt was not destructive; it created a good feeling.

Other times you are facing an Event and, rather than trusting your feelings, you doubt yourself and start worrying with the "what if" games. When this happens, you bring negative emotions to the Event, and those negative emotions control the Choice you make. As you implement your Choice, you are filled with worry, doubt, uncertainty, negative fear, which causes you to only see the bad you perceive is going to happen. The result is mental confusion, emotional uncertainty and physical exhaustion. That leaves you reeling with negative feelings. You are uptight; you are a hostage to your fear; your emotions are beating you down; your mind is shut out; your body is worn out. This is negative stress being created by what you are feeling.

It is important you understand *those feelings are expressed through behavior*. For many this is just another increase in the negative stress. When they are asked, "How are you doing?" their response is not truthful. "Oh, I'm doing okay." Reality is—*they are not doing okay*. They are on a destructive collision course with self. Too many times those collisions are not dents and scratches; those personal collisions can total their life.

I am a firm believer that most of the mental, emotional and physical illness people deal with is the result of negative stress controlling their life. Rather than being honest with self and admitting they need help, they lie to self and continue on a destructive path. For some reason they feel if they admit they have stress, they will be viewed as weak, or as a person who can't take care of self. Reality is *none of us can take care of ourselves all the time*. All of us go through times when we need to reach out and ask for guidance. It is not a sign of weakness; it is actually a sign of strength.

As much as many believe *they are self sufficient*, they are not. During your time on this earth, you will need help. During your life, there will be times when life hands you more than you can handle on your own. If you are so insecure you can't ask for help, you will shorten the life span you have.

This reveals one of the most important issues surrounding negative stress. *The weaker your foundation of self worth the more negative stress you will have in your life.* Most who tell you they are confident and in control of their life are really driven by the moment and lack the confidence it takes to get through the shifting sand of living.

Negative stress feeds off of your lack of self-worth, which affects your self-trust. The lack of self-trust creates most of your moments of personal doubt and personal fear. Negative stress attacks you through making you doubt yourself and only see the bad that could happen. Once you begin that journey, your greatest challenge becomes redesigning your behaviors. You are not what you say; you are what you demonstrate through your behavior.

When you can't be honest about you, you are trapped in a world that keeps you colliding with yourself. Each collision does more damage to your foundation of self-worth and moves you further away from being able to live a healthy life.

For years I have watched people lie to self and refuse to face the behaviors that are pushing them deeper into a life of confusion, depression and self-destruction.

I want to say to them, "You don't have to live this way. Slow down and examine the emotions you are using to define who you are. Wake up and see the other side. Step away from the self-destructive behavior you are using. Get free to experience the joy and fulfillment you were put here to experience."

The tragedy is many have lived this way so long they don't believe there is another side. They have given up, settled and exist every day destroying self from the inside out.

It is for these people that I write this book as a sense of hope. If you can see what you are doing through the lives of others who have traveled your journey, BUT faced their behavior and turned it around, you can be free of the self-destructive life you're living through negative stress.

This book is for the talented people who have gotten

down on self. You don't have to settle; you are free to live your life to the max, BUT until you change the behavior that is giving negative stress control of your life, you will remain trapped in your world of self-limiting behavior. Learn from the stories of these pages. Put yourself in the place of the people in this book and allow their success to give you the inner strength to break free of your negative stress.

This book is for the masses who every day view life from all the negative that is thrown at them. September 11, 2001 will go down in history as the day that changed our lives forever. If the terrorists wanted to instill fear, they did it. If the terrorists wanted to send an emotional shock wave through this country, they achieved it. 9/11 took the stress level of this country to the red zone. People found themselves dealing with emotions they had never dealt with before. They found themselves emotionally paralyzed. They struggled to understand why this happened and feared it was just the beginning of terrible things to come.

We are now time and distance away from that event, and the effects are still emotionally affecting people. The emotional scars of 9/11 are not healed and still have the ability to push people into a negative world filled with "what if." That game feeds our negative side and results in an increase in our negative stress.

I wish the media could be held responsible for the emotional damage they do to people. Yes, they have the responsibility of reporting the news, BUT there are many different ways to present information. The shock approach, the fear they use, the lack of sensitivity they approach things with makes them partially responsible for the increase in negative stress many are dealing with today.

It is dangerous to give a group the license to do what they want to do without being held accountable for their behavior. There are a lot of ethical wrongs here, and the powers to be are fearful of standing up and holding the media accountable for their behavior. The media is one of the largest stressors we have.

If the purpose of terrorism is to inflict confusion and fear through behavior whether spoken, written or physical, would some media groups fit this descriptive plan? Our society has enough people being controlled by negative stress. They don't need those given the responsibility of presenting truth a free license to do it through a negative presentation. Frightening people to improve ratings makes an ethical statement about their real mission.

Stress is a fact! If you are alive, you deal with it on a daily basis. That's okay; that's a part of life. The danger is allowing the events of life to gather negative emotions and turn something that was not meant to be dangerous into a disease that can kill you.

Learn from the pages of this book how to control your daily stress. Learn from the stories of people who are just like you and have had to grow in their understanding of how to manage their life, rather than allowing their life to manage them.

Building Blocks For Controlling Stress is a book written for you, about you and designed to help you have the best life possible by living a life filled with positive stress.

# Just Eliminate It!

*People who work to eliminate stress become stressful; people who learn to control their stress enhance their creativity.*

I was packing my equipment when he approached me. He reached out his hand and said, "Do I know you?"

I stopped, looked at him, shook his hand and responded, "I don't think we have ever met."

"Then, how do you know so much about me? I could swear you have been living in my life for the last three years. Everything you said was my life."

There was a long pause as he gathered himself. I could tell he needed my ears, so I motioned for him to sit down. He pulled a chair up to the table where my equipment was, sat down and placed his head in his hands. "My life hasn't been worth a flip for the past three years."

I waited as he took deep breath and leaned back in his chair. It was apparent this wasn't easy for him and the last thing he needed was for me to ask him any questions. This was his conversation, and it needed to happen at his pace.

"I have been such a fool. I have been so selfish. My behavior has destroyed everything that was important to me. I don't have a room in my life that isn't upside down. I listened as you talked about the rooms of your life and realized I don't have a house. I have a pile of rubbish."

His look told me he was asking for permission to continue. I leaned back and responded, "What happened to your house?"

"Well, it all started in my business room. That was my living room. It was all I had time for. I didn't need to be there as much as I was, but I made it okay by telling myself

The desire to eliminate
something out of your life
is just another form of
avoidance behavior.

I was doing it for my family. That was a lie; I was doing it to stay away from my family. Oh, don't get me wrong. I love my family. It was just all the noise and confusion that went on at home. I just couldn't handle it, so I ran away to my business."

He paused to reflect on what he was saying, took another deep breath and continued. "The irony of it was I didn't accomplish anything while I was supposedly doing business. All I did was create more stress for myself and all those who were there to help me. When they couldn't stand it, they left. That just made the stress worse. Now, I had my work and theirs to do. Rather than step up and face what was happening, I blamed them for the mess I was in."

The look on his face turned from disgust to pain. "I would take that anger home and my wife and kids got the blunt of it. I would go home, sit at the table in silence and then go into my home office and stay there until I was so tired I couldn't keep my eyes open. Many nights I would just sleep on the couch. My wife would try to talk to me, and I would just yell at her to leave me alone. My kids would try to be with me, and I would push them away. I became a monster at home and finally Sarah couldn't take it anymore. I came home one day, and they were all gone. When I found them, they were at her mother's house. Sarah told me she couldn't take my behavior anymore. I was destroying her and the kids. She told me she wanted the relationship to work, but if I couldn't get my act together, she would divorce me. She gave me three months to get myself together."

The long pause that followed told me he was replaying that tape in his mind. "I've got to tell you all that did was make me more angry. I told myself if she really loved me she would understand all I was going through and be there to support me.

I wouldn't allow this to be my problem. I was busting my butt for them."

He paused again and chuckled out loud. "Sounded good at the moment, but inside I knew it was a lie. Blaming them didn't make me the bad guy. What a crock! It was just another lie designed to make someone else responsible for my life."

The smile disappeared and the look of pain returned. "You talked about a social room. I don't have one. People don't want to be around me. I am nothing but a pile of negative junk. I have told myself I don't need people, but the reality is I am so tired of being alone. I want friends, but the people who want to be my friend are just like me. Being around them is like being with me. That is not fun! All we do is feed each other's negative stress. You talked about a personal room. That thought is so frightening to me. You said that was a place where you go to be by yourself. That is the most uncomfortable thought I have. I don't want to be with me; I don't like being with me; I try to avoid being alone with me. I am not a good person."

When I heard him say he was not a good person, I stopped him. "Wait a minute. Are you hearing what you are saying? You are sitting here continuing your journey of beating yourself down, which is feeding your negative stress in your life. You are a good person. You have just allowed your life to get out of control. You have to stop this negative journey and get yourself prepared to think about the good in your life."

"Good in my life! There is no good in my life. Believe me when I tell you I have come close to ending this mess I have created. I didn't have the guts to do it."

"There is always good in a life. On the worst day you will ever have there is still good happening. The truth is you are so lost in your pain you can't see the good. It is there, but

JUST ELIMINATE IT!

you have lost the ability to see it."

"Can you help me eliminate all this negative crap I have brought into my life?"

"No!"

My response took him by surprise. "I don't understand. I thought you were a person who wanted to help people."

"I am, BUT your choice of words makes it impossible for me to be of any help to you."

That created even more confusion for him. The look said he was lost.

"I don't understand what you are talking about. All I am doing is asking you to help me."

"No! That is not what you said. You asked me to help you eliminate the negative stress from your life. You can't eliminate it. To eliminate it means to erase all that has been from your memory. That can't happen. When you work to eliminate the negative of the past from your present, all you do is increase its presence in your life. That means you are working harder to stress yourself more."

Now, I had his attention. "What you are saying makes sense, but I don't understand what you are saying."

As strange as his words may have sounded, I knew exactly what he was saying.

"Mack, you are wanting to get rid of all this without facing any of it. That doesn't work. Improvement always starts with facing what is. That means slowing down, looking at your behavior and understanding why and how you have made it okay. You can't erase what has been, BUT you can redesign the behavior you have used to make it okay."

His posture told me I needed to slow down. He was struggling to stay up with what I was saying.

"Listen to what I am telling you. The desire to eliminate

13

anything out of your life is just another form of avoidance behavior. When you work to eliminate anything, it says you do not want to face it. Nothing can improve without facing what has been. Why do you think so many people just keep repeating those things that create their stress? They don't face what they have done; they try to throw it away, and it just moves to their internal storage unit. It is not gone; it is laying there waiting to happen all over again."

"Is that why I just keep doing the same dumb things over and over? I mean I do it and tell myself that was dumb and that I am not going to do it again. I am not really dealing with it; I am avoiding it and then repeating it."

"That's right. Remember what I said about a definition of stress. *Stress is anything in your life that makes you uptight.* When you get uptight, you tend to emotionally avoid. When you avoid, you set yourself up for repeating the behavior. That is why it is so important for people to understand my statement—*People who work to eliminate stress become stressful; those who learn to control their stress enhance their creativity.*

To reduce the negative stress in your life you must face the behaviors that have created it. If you work to eliminate the stress, you are only increasing it. The next time you have to deal with a like situation you will find your anxiety and all its negative family members stronger in your life. If you face the stress when it is happening, you increase your mental creativity and rather than store, you release the stress. Now, you are in control of your life."

"Where were you three years ago? All I have been doing is increasing the pressure in my life. I guess I really haven't dealt with anything. I only hope I can go back and rebuild what I have worked so hard to destroy."

Mack and I have slowly worked through his behaviors and have faced each of them. Today his business is growing, his wife and kids are back with him and his behavior is designed to respond to life as it is happening, not react after he has messed things up.

Are you in anyway like Mack? Most could be his twin. It's too easy to just avoid facing what is happening in your life. Reality is *that just feeds your negative stress.*

Avoidance behavior is a negative way of running from what you fear. You don't run because you don't understand; you run because you don't want to face "what is." When you run, you give the situation a bigger presence in your life. That means rather than things getting resolved, they just grow by attaching more negative emotions.

Now, what do you think that will do to your stress level? How many times do you choose to avoid, rather than confront? How many times have you given yourself permission to walk away, rather than step up and face the issue?

Stress is not bad, until you work to avoid the pressure it is causing in your life. When you avoid, you turn the good to bad. The result is you lacking the inner strength to move forward. Remember, *negative stress keeps you trapped in the circle of repetitive behavior.*

**How Do You Learn To Control The Stress In Your Life?**
    S    start by facing what you are doing
    T    trust yourself to handle it
    R    refuse to run away
    E    emotionally slow down
    S    stay focused on resolving the issue
    S    seek outside help

## THE ORIGIN
*Stress is the result of emotions, not the events in your life.*

Stress is a fact! When you avoid the stress pockets in your life, you are actually increasing them. Those two thoughts are critical to you living a life filled with positive stress and not allowing the negative destructive side of stress to gain control of you. Once the negative side of stress is imbedded in your life, you will have a tremendous emotional challenge getting beyond it.

In the introduction to this book I discussed with you the concept of:
- *Event*
- *Feeling*
- *Choice*

The greatest challenge for most is understanding where the stress came from. It seems so confusing when you know you are wrestling with something that is turning your life upside down, but you have no idea where it is coming from. The result is you spending time and money doing things that don't provide you with a solution. What does that do? It only adds to your stress and heightens the anxiety you are feeling. I was speaking in Atlanta when Peter and Ann approached me. I returned to our product table after finishing a walk around with a young lady who had needed a few minutes with me. Karen walked over, pointed to a young couple and said, "They really need to talk to you."

I walked over to where they were seated, pulled out a chair and said, "So, we need to talk?"

Peter looked at me and instantly I could see the mixture

17

Don't underestimate the ability of your old negative tapes to increase your stress and hold you a hostage within your own body.

of pain and anger in his eyes. "Richard, I am probably the most angry person you have ever met. I feel like I have this fire inside me and I can't put it out. I don't like this person I am. I am punishing everyone in my life. I punish Ann; I punish our children; I punish my customers, BUT most of all I am punishing myself."

He paused, and I knew he was waiting for me to jump in. I leaned back, looked at the two of them and asked Ann, "Is this a pretty good description of him?"

With tears in her eyes she looked at me and said, "Yes! He is so angry. I have known him for twelve years and the anger has just gotten worse. In the beginning we would joke about it."

She paused, looked at Peter, took his hand and continued while she was looking at him. "When we were dating, he would lose his temper, but it was no big deal. He would blow up and then return to his happy go lucky self. Lately, all that has changed. His anger isn't for a moment. Richard, it is a continual thing, and I am very scared."

I interrupted her to ask, "Scared for who?"

"For me and the kids. He comes home from work and immediately starts screaming at the kids. Nothing I do is right. It is as if he is looking for some reason to go off on me. I don't know how much longer I can take this. There are days I think I should just pack up and leave while he is at work. Yet, if I do that, I am fearful it will just fuel his anger."

"Peter, do you think you would ever hurt your family?"

"I can tell you no, but I am not sure. This anger is so strong inside of me I am not sure what I will do. I find myself driving and someone cuts in front of me, and I think if I had a gun, I would just pull up in front of them and shoot them."

"Do you think you are capable of doing that?"

"I don't know. I don't think so, but I don't know."

"Have you been to a doctor about your anger?"

They looked at each other, and Peter just started laughing. "Yes, I have been to several doctors. They listen to my story and want to give me drugs to control my anger. I am taking medication now, but it isn't helping. I have got to get beyond this. I can't live this way. This fire inside of me just keeps burning hotter and hotter. Can you help me?"

Peter is a great illustration of Event, Feelings and Choice. The challenge Peter faced was understanding where this anger was coming from and what was feeding its fire.

During the next few months, Peter, Ann and I worked to control his anger. It was not an easy journey for him, but he wanted to get beyond this so strongly he was willing to go through the pain.

During our time together, we were able to isolate several stressors that were feeding his anger.

Before we go on it is important you understand the term "stressor." A stressor is a connection point for the feelings you are having. Too many want to deal with the feelings without finding the connection point. If you deal with the feelings and never find the connection point (stressor), you are only creating moments. You are not helping control the flow of emotions that are causing the increased stress. When you can find the connecting point, you can redesign the feelings, which in turn will allow you to control the emotions. When the emotions are controlled, you allow yourself the freedom to make different choices.

Here is what we found as connection points for Peter's anger:

- During his childhood, his dad never had time for him. He grew up feeling no one loved him.

- His dad left and left his mother with the kids. All she had time for was work. Peter and his brothers raised themselves. There was no time for play; they worked to make money for the family.

- When Peter's dad did walk back into his life, he acted like nothing had ever happened. Peter tried to talk to his dad, but his dad brushed him off.

- Peter took all those emotions he had and buried them.

- When Peter and Ann met, she made him feel very special. She offered him what he didn't get from his childhood — time and love.

- Peter didn't pay much attention to his mother. He only had eyes for Ann — who was becoming the parent he never had.

- Once they got married, all that changed. Ann turned from Peter back to her mother. Her mother didn't like Peter, so every time she and Ann were together she would talk negative about Peter.

- That effected Ann's view of Peter and she started beating Peter with all the negative stuff her mother had said to her.

Can you see where all this is going? It was like Peter

was trapped in this vicious negative circle. What he had been looking for he thought he had found in Ann, BUT once they got married he found himself in a continuation of the circle he was trying to get out of. All the anger he had stored toward his father and his mother was now free to come out.

Yes, in the beginning of their relationship he was able to keep the anger buried. Yes, there were times when it got out, but he was always able to push it back into its closet. Why? Because he had found what he thought he had been searching for in life — love and acceptance. He had found a parent. Then, when he started experiencing the negative behavior from Ann, the inner closet came open and all the anger came racing out. The icing on the cake was the anger didn't come by itself. All the other emotions that were attached to the anger came rushing out and joined in the attack.

With this as a backdrop let's see if we can tie this to the idea of Event, Feelings and Choice. Each of these three is present, but to understand the origin of the stress you have to understand the role each of these three play.

EVENT: If you go back to Peter's childhood, all the old tapes he made about his father created a point of connection for his emotions. The behavior of his father became the stressor that would feed Peter for years to come.

FEELINGS: The experience with his father triggered an emotional journey for Peter. With each Event your life is handed there will be the attachment of the emotions. Put the emotions together with your mind and you get feelings. If the emotions have a stronger presence than your mind, the result is a negative definition. If your mental presence is stronger than your emotions, you get a positive definition. The key is which of the two has the stronger presence. In Peter's situation his emotions had the stronger presence. The result was an inner vault of unresolved negative feelings.

As Peter grew with these unresolved emotions they began to find their way into the other areas of his life. Their presence began the pathway he used to understand the other Events his life was handed.

CHOICES: Anytime you put Feelings with an Event you will make a Choice. The Choice becomes the behavior you demonstrate through action.

Each time Peter came face to face with an Event that reminded him of his childhood those unresolved feelings triggered certain behaviors. In this case the major emotion was anger, and the standard behavior was to attack those around his life.

If those Emotions are not addressed, they increase in power. The more powerful the emotions the less you listen to your mind. The weaker your mental presence the more reactive you become. As your reactive nature grows, you lose control of your rational side. When that happens, you are driven by your negative perceptions, rather than your desire to resolve and move beyond those dangerous emotions. Now, I am not saying you totally give in to the negative emotions. There will be times when your desire to get beyond is strong, but because your negative emotions have become the guide for your life, you tend to give into the pressure to stay the same.

This is the biggest battle most people face in their life. *The stronger the battle the greater the pressure you are under.*

Most underestimate the power of their negative feelings. Most feel once those feelings are exposed, you just tell yourself you are not going to give into them anymore and the battle is over. WRONG!

Peter put it this way. "I didn't think it was going to be this tough. I figured once I understood what was happening it would be a piece of cake. WOW! Was I wrong. The more I understand the more difficult the journey."

Peter and I had been working together for four months when I received a phone call from Ann. As I was playing the message, I could hear the desperation in her voice.

"Richard, this is Ann. I need for you to call me as soon as possible. I don't know what is happening to Peter, but he is out of control. For the first time in a long time he scared me this morning. The look in his eyes frightened me. Please call me."

I called and was able to reach her. "Ann, this is Richard. What's going on with Peter?"

"You know the doctor gave him some new medication."

One of the things I had Peter do was have a long talk with his doctor about the medication he had been placed on. Peter is a big guy and the medication he was on was not strong enough to control his emotions. I am not a big believer in pills, but in some situations you need them to create the calmness necessary to face the issue. With Peter this medicine was necessary.

"Yes, and we talked about the adjustment time it was going to take for it to work."

"How long do you think that will be? He is out of control."

"Define out of control for me."

"Well, in the past he was able to somewhat control his anger. For the past couple of days it seems he can't control it. He lashes out at me for no reason; he screams at the kids because they are making too much noise. Richard, they are simply being kids. I am glad when he goes into his study and shuts the door. In there he will calm down, but I never know which Peter is going to come out."

"Okay Ann, let's go back over what we talked about. With this new medication Peter is going to have an emotional turn over time. While this is happening and he is adjusting to it, there is going to be a time where the angry Peter is going to be ugly. This will cease, but you are going to have to be patient. I know it is not easy, but these attacks will subside. Have Peter call his doctor and explain what is happening."

What was happening was the increase in attacks by the Old Angry Peter. That ugly person knew Peter was serious about locking him away and used the medicine change over time to increase his attacks. The increase in attacks strengthened Peter's feelings, which in turn fed the outburst of his anger.

Today Peter is doing much better. His emotions have adjusted to the new medication and each conversation we have is moving him closer to resolving his anger connection points. There are times when I can sense his stress level rising. I understand these are the times when his negative emotions are raising their ugly head and striving to break free. When those times happen, we slow everything down even further and address why the attack is happening at this moment.

Ann has also stepped up her presence. She is more aware of which of her behaviors feeds Peter's anger. She is beginning to understand she has many of her mother's negative traits and has to be aware of when those behaviors are coming to the surface. She understands those behaviors trigger old tapes in Peter which feeds his anger.

Working through this situation is not just Peter's issue.

It is Peter and Ann working together. If and when Ann feeds Peter's anger, she becomes a stressor in his life. She needs to be part of the solution, not a trigger for the anger. Both have to slow down and face emotionally what they are bringing to the relationship.

Does the story of Peter and Ann make sense to you? Can you see how Events become the triggers; how Feelings create the table you feast at and when the two are put together, they create the Choices you make that are acted out through behavior.

Out of control these three, Events, Feelings and Choices, create a dangerous pathway. When these three are under control, they allow you to move forward seeking resolution, rather than feeding your negative emotions.

Don't forget — all emotions have two sides. There is a positive and a negative side to each emotion. The Choices you implement through behavior are the result of which side of the emotion you are allowing to take control of the Event you are facing. That is why the slower you move emotionally the less negative stress you are going to have in your life.

Stress is a fact! You are not going to live without it, but you can live controlling the impact it has on your life mentally, emotionally and physically.

**To Stay On The Positive Side Of Your Emotions You Must:**
P    pace yourself
O    open yourself to truth
S    stay focused on resolving the event
I    invest in learning about you
T    talk to yourself out loud
I    if necessary, seek outside help
V    validate positive actions
E    express your true feelings

# FULL HOUSE

*Stress in any one room of your life will find its way into all the rooms of your life.*

More than anything, Ruth wanted a relationship. She wanted someone in her life who would love her; someone who would take care of her; someone who would make her feel like a queen.

She had had relationships before, but they had come apart when there was pressure to slow down her Business Room. Each time her Business Room collided with her Family Room, she would react and retreat deeper into her Business Room. The result would be the guy feeling rejection and moving out of her life.

When that happened, her Business Room was thrown into a tailspin. For weeks there would be confusion and an increase in her personal stress. That stress got dumped on all who worked for her.

The office joke became "Get ready. Ruth has ended another relationship, and we are going to get the blunt of it." The tragedy was it cost her some very talented people. They refused to be part of her personal pain that got dumped on them.

"I just don't understand what is happening," were her opening words to me.

I had done a program on *Balancing Work and Home*, and she was the first one to get to me.

"You and I have to talk," were the words coming out of her mouth as she was looking at me with eyes screaming for help.

"You were speaking to me today. I am the person you

27

Anyone who is running
from anything is living a life
where they are increasing
their negative stress.

defined as "dangerous. I have no balance in my life. When I look at your four rooms, I realize I live in a one-room house, and that's my Business Room. I want a relationship more than anything, but each time I find myself torn between my Business Room and my Family Room. I think if someone really loves me, they will understand the importance of my Business Room. Do you think I am wrong about that?"

"Ruth, people who care about you want to know that they matter. That means when you are with them they want to feel they are the most important thing in your life. They don't want to fight your Business Room to have time with you. They want you to turn it off and pay attention to them. When you can't, they question whether they really matter to your life. Do you understand that?"

"Yes! I understand what you are saying. It is just for some reason I can't let go of my Business Room. I need your help here. I really do want this balance. I realize without it I will never have a long term healthy relationship."

There are so many Ruth's out there. They are both male and female. Their life is one-dimensional. They think they have their life together, but reality is there is no balance to their life. Without balance there is constant tiredness. That tiredness steals the energy needed to complete events. Each incomplete event increases your stress. Each time you think about the situation or strive to find the time you don't have, it creates this inner feeling of being uptight. Remember, *stress is anything in life that makes you feel uptight.*

Balance is not about having control of one room of your life. Balance is about having a living design where all four of your rooms are working together to support each of the other rooms. Let's briefly look at these four rooms.

The largest room in 99% of all people's lives is their Business Room. It is large because of all the things it offers the rest of your life. The money the Business Room provides creates much of what the other rooms will achieve. This makes most feel this is the most important room in their life. Reality is, *it isn't!*

Most men and career women define who they are through their Business Room. If you ask them, "Who are you?" they will answer with what they do in their Business Room.

Yes, the Business Room is important, but when it is overstated or misused, it creates a lot of negative stress for the rest of your life.

Ron came to me because he felt his family didn't understand why he spent so much time in his Business Room. "Richard, they just don't get it. They think I enjoy spending all my time doing business. I don't, but if I don't spend the time there, there isn't the money for the things they want to do. I have tried to tell my wife, but she just doesn't get it. She wants me to be home for dinner with the kids. I can't do that and achieve all I want to achieve. I can't be at their baseball or soccer games and stay caught up at work. The kids are young and don't understand what my business demands of me. They are too young to see that all the perks they will have in their life will be because of what I achieve in my Business Room. Can you help me explain it to my family?"

"Ron, I can't help you explain it to them when I don't agree with what you are doing. When the things of life are taking you away from those who love you, you need to reexamine your priorities. You only have a certain amount of time with your kids. Miss that time, and they grow up without a healthy definition of a father. Is that what you want for them?

You wife has the right to expect you to be part of the family. If your life-style demands you work all the time, you need to examine your life-style. Time is not something you can miss and then make up. It comes and it goes and you cannot go back and have the parts of it you have missed."

Too many use business as the reason they don't have a presence in their Family Room. These two rooms must work together to support the journey you are on. When they don't support each other, there is constant conflict. That conflict wears on all the people involved. That wearing will increase the negative tension between people. That means negative stress attacks people from the inside out.

This means pressure in the Business Room will find its way into the Family Room. Pressure in the Family Room will find its way into the Business Room. Anyone in either of these rooms will feel the tension coming from the other room.

When the wearing starts to happen, it steals the most important thing the Family Room offers those who share the room — a feeling of love and support.

Time and time again I have sat in the counseling room listening to couples share the destruction of their Family Room, I have heard them talk about the lack of time, the lack of presence and the lack of connection. When that happens, those who share the room become strangers who hang out, not share quality togetherness. The result is an increase in the tension between the people. That will feed the negative stress and pull people apart.

The third room is your Social Room. The purpose of this room is fun and relaxation. It is where you go to unwind, laugh and have fun with people you enjoy. Too many don't have this room, or if they do have it, it is used for the wrong reason.

This room has become the #1 room of escape. People don't go there to unwind; they go to hide. Rather than this room being a stress release, it has become a stress creator. Anyone who is running from anything is living a life where they are increasing their negative stress. The things you are avoiding are simply feeding the negative stress in your life.

Why do you think people drink to the excess, or do drugs? Do you think they do it for the fun? No! They do it to escape facing self. Any person who uses any substance to the point of abuse does not do it by accident. It is behavior designed to run away from the person they don't want to face. The #1 room for achieving this has become the Social Room. Why? Because there are always people there who are doing the same thing and will validate what you are doing. This self-destructive behavior just feeds all your negative emotions, which increases your negative stress.

Then, there is your Personal Room. If you study most people's life design, this is the missing room. It's always apparent which life is out of control. All you have to do is notice there is no time for self. Their life is all about catching up; it is about taking care of others; it is about trying to please everyone else. It is about never having time to do what they want to do. They are always the last one on their list.

Have you ever resented what others asked you to do, or what they expected you to do for them? Have you ever wanted to just run away and not be there to take care of them? That is the result of having no Personal Room in your life.

The Personal Room is where you go to be with you. No one can go with you. If they do, it becomes a Social Room.

The Personal Room is the most important room in your life. It is more important than your Business Room; it is more important than your Family Room; it is more important than your Social Room.

It is the most important room in your life because it is where your dreams are created. All the things you will achieve in the other rooms of your life will have their origin in your Personal Room. When there is no time for you, your creativity decreases. When there is no time for you, there will always be confusion in the other rooms. The lack of a Personal Room is the major reason there is negative stress in the other rooms of your life.

It is the most important room in your life because in this room lives the real you. The "you" that others see is, in most cases, may not be the real you. Most people have multiple personalities. They learn at an early age to play the game of *being who they need to be*. That game becomes a life-style, and only when alone with self are they the real deal.

It is the most important room because it is the only place where there is really time for you. If there is no personal time for you, you tend to resent what others want you to become. That will increase your stress and make you more resentful.

It is the most important room because it is where you learn to control your pockets of unhealthy stress. The Personal Room is the only place where you can slow down and move at a pace you can manage. Without a Personal Room you will lack control in the other rooms of your life. That means confusion in one room will find its way into the other rooms in your life. When the confusion spreads, you find yourself not wanting to spend time in any of the rooms in your life. Now, what do you think that will do to your stress level? What happens when there is no place to go without feeling overwhelmed or overstressed?

When these rooms are in order and working together, there is balance in your life. When they are colliding with each other, you will constantly be guided by worry, doubt and the desire to get your life back in sync. The challenge will be redesigning the rooms of your life with the correct order.

*To control your stress the order must be:*
- Personal Room
- Family/Relationship Room
- Business Room
- Social Room

Redesigning will demand a reformatting of your priorities. It will require you making some major decisions. Many of which will not be comfortable. You will know the redesigning is correct, but old habits are challenging to break. You can do it for a while, but for most they slip back into the old routines that have driven their life for years. That becomes fodder for their negative stress.

Redesigning will mean eliminating some things from your life. There are behaviors you have used to justify your unhealthy stressful design. Redesigning will demand the removal of those behaviors. As long as they are still in place, you will have a reason to go backward. Each time you step back to where you were, you validate yesterday and increase the negative stress in today.

It will mean confronting people whose presence has fed your negative stress. This creates a major challenge for most. One man put it this way. "It will be easier to wait for them to die than have that conversation with them."

Much of your negative stress is the result of conflict in your rooms that has never been resolved. This unresolved conflict makes the room a tension center, and since most don't like conflict, the easy way out is to just avoid the room. The truth is it just strengthens the negative stress and redesigns the rest of your rooms with unhealthy relics.

Without balance your life will always be in turmoil. Without balance you will always be running from something. Without balance your rooms will be tied together with tension, rather than joy.

Stress is a fact! Stress that is not faced and controlled will find its way into every nook and cranny of your life. That is not healthy living.

**To Achieve Balance In Your Life You Must:**

B    begin by evaluating your rooms
A    acknowledge the stressors in each room
L    list the confusion the stressors create
A    address the stressors with the people
N    new guidelines are created
C    common agendas are put in place
E    each person steps up through behavior

## FEAR AND STRESS
*Negative fear is the root cause of most of your negative stress.*

Just as stress is a fact, so is fear. Of all the emotions you will ever wrestle with fear is the second largest. 99% of all your worries, your frustrations, your uncertainties, and your negative behaviors can be tied to your fears.

Like any emotion, fear has a positive and a negative side. The place fear plays in your life depends on which aspect of fear you give control.

When positive fear is guiding your life, you slow down, look at things through a sensible approach and handle them in a constructive fashion.

When negative fear is guiding your life, you speed up, sees things that don't exist, turn to the wrong people and just want this to be over. This doesn't allow you to address issues; it forces you to avoid issues and stockpile them in your life. The more you stockpile the greater your negative stress.

In my years of working with human behavior I have found this to be one of the greatest prison cells most live in. Rather than facing and working through issues, people internally store them in their emotional vault. They don't understand what that does to their life. Anything you store keeps reappearing in different forms in your life.

Ron's question to me was simply, "Why can't I get beyond this in my life?"

He was in his mid 30's, very talented, well established, BUT totally stressed. Years before I had helped his dad through a rough transition time in his life. When Ron learned I was back in the Palm Beaches, he sought me out. We met at Testa's, one of my favorite Palm Beach restaurants, for breakfast. I

When you get down on yourself you are a candidate for negative fear to attack. That will increase your negative stress.

wasn't sure if I would recognize him. He was only a little tot when I had worked with his father. When I arrived at the restaurant, he wasn't hard to spot. I looked around; saw this guy who looked like he had not slept in weeks, sitting at this table with a pencil in his hand he was using to peck on the table with.

When he saw me, he was immediately out of his chair and on his way toward me. With his hand stretched out he said, "Richard, thank you for making time to see me. I didn't know if you would have time to fit me into your schedule. I really need your help."

As we sat down, I asked him, "How is your dad?"

"Dad is great. He said to tell you hello. He was the one that suggested I call you. Someone you played golf with told him you were back. He told me if anyone could help me, it would be you."

"I appreciate your father's trust in me, but I am not a miracle worker. Why don't you tell me what is going on in your life."

"My life! That's the problem. I don't have a life. All I have is this huge pocket of problems packed on top of problems. Richard, I am mentally, emotionally and physically worn out."

"Start at the beginning and tell me what has happened."

"You know my dad and you know how driven and forceful he can be. Since childhood, he has been preparing me to take over his business. At first I thought it would be fun, but when the time came for me to step into the business, I found myself not wanting that as my life. The more dad talked about my involvement, the greater my stress level. It got so bad I got sick. I went to the doctor and the first question he asked was *what is going on in your life?* I told him and he suggested I talk to dad."

"Did you?"

"Are you kidding! Tell my dad I didn't want to take over the business he has spent 35 years preparing for me. Do you know what that would do to him? Do you know how he would have reacted? I didn't and still don't have the guts to have that conversation with him. I don't know what I am going to do. I am 33 and on blood pressure medicine. I don't sleep; I don't eat right; my wife is threatening to leave me if I don't get this worked out. I don't know what to do or where to turn. There are days I think it would be easier to just die."

There was a pause as he gathered himself emotionally. "I know what you are going to tell me. I need to talk to dad and tell him what I am feeling."

There was another pause and he drifted off into a moment of deep thought. He looked back at me with a look of terror in his eyes. "I am just too frightened to have that conversation with him. It would kill him to know I don't want to be in the family business, nor do I want to take it over. It would just kill him. I can't do that to him."

"Ron, first of all, I don't think it would kill him. Your dad is smart enough to know something is wrong. Does he ever question you?"

"All the time. He is constantly wanting to know if I am okay. He is constantly questioning me about things at home. He wants to know if Shelly and I are doing okay. Mom has even mentioned how much weight I have lost and wants to know if I am all right. I have thought about talking to her and asking her to talk to dad for me, but that is not fair to her. I don't know what to do."

"Ron, let me say this to you one more time. I don't think the conversation would kill your father. Granted, he won't be happy, but with all he has been through he would understand. With what I know about your father, he wouldn't want you to be part of something you don't want to be part of."

I paused to let the words sink in and then continued. "Second, if you don't face this fear and address this issue, you are going to kill yourself. The negative stress you are living with is not healthy. This is the type of stress that causes heart disease. Look at you! You are wearing yourself out from all the stress you are struggling with. What fear is keeping you from addressing this with your father?"

The look on his face told me this was the major issue. "There are two. The first is the fear of letting him down. You know he wanted both Stan and I to be his partners. When Stan died in the car crash, all those hopes and plans were transferred to me. He still talks about how Stan and I together would have been the perfect business partners. I am so afraid if I tell him I don't want to be in the business, it will emotionally destroy him. I couldn't live with myself if I did that to him."

"Ron, don't you think your dad knows you aren't happy? Don't you think he is worried about you?"

"Yes, I know he is worried, BUT he thinks my unhappiness is about Shelly and I. I don't think he has any idea of how unhappy I am with the job."

"You said there were two fears. What is the other fear you are wrestling with?"

"It's the fear of him not liking me anymore. I love my dad, and I want my dad to love me. I want him to be proud of me. I know how important the business is to him. He comes into my office all the time to talk about the future of the

41

business and about how I am going to take this business to
another level. I can feel his excitement. I have learned how
to fake the excitement with him. I don't want him not to love
me, and I am fearful if I tell him I don't want to work in the
business, he won't love me anymore."

"Ron, I don't think your father's love is conditioned
on whether you are in the business or not. I know your father
well enough to know how much he loves you. Again, he will
be disappointed with your decision, but his disappointment will
not cause him to stop loving you."

"In my heart I know you are right, but I can't bring
myself to tell him. I can't go on living this lie. The pressure in
my life is too great; the damage it is doing to my family is too
much. Each day that passes puts more pressure on me. I have
got to get rid of this stress, before it gets rid of me."

"Hey, I have an idea. Why don't we both talk to your
father? I will not have the conversation for you, but I will be
there with you."

"You would do that for me?"

"Yes! This has got to be handled quickly. It has the
potential of destroying too many lives. You set it up, let me
know and I will be there with you."

Two days later we met with his dad. It was not easy
for Ron to have the conversation, but he did a good job of
explaining to his dad his real dream.

The words back to Ron from his father were, "Son,
why didn't you tell me this sooner? I just want you to be happy
in your life. Don't do things because you think that is what I
want. Live your life to be you."

Negative fear has such a damaging effect on your life.
There are so many who live like Ron. There are things in

their life they need to address, but the fear of addressing them takes over and controls the decisions of their life. The result is mental, emotional and physical damage.

Negative fear attacks you at the level of your self-trust. It makes you doubt yourself. Doubt is one of those emotions that wears you down. The greater the doubt the greater the emotional drain on your total person.

Negative fear makes you play the "what if" game. This is such a dangerous game. It makes you question each and every thing you do. There is no time to relax; every aspect of your life is under the microscope and you end up looking at the wrongs, rather than searching for the good. That is so exhausting. It just increases the negative stress in your life.

Negative fear makes you listen to the wrong people. Have you ever gone through a down time in your life and out of the woodwork comes all these negative people. You look around and wonder, "Where they came from?" They have always been there, but you weren't paying attention to them. Then, when your life is upside down and your defenses are down, you start listening to them. They are not there to help you; they are there to keep you down and hopefully out.

Look at negative from any angle you want to and its power will always come back to one issue -- a crack in your foundation of self worth. People who have a solid foundation of self worth don't wrestle with negative fear. Now, don't hear what I am not saying. Yes, it is still present in their life, but they don't wrestle with it. Their self-trust is strong enough to see beyond the negative and focus on the good. That means the negative fear cannot increase the negative stress. Learn this and learn it well.

*When you are down on yourself, you are a candidate for negative fear which will increase the negative stress.*

**How Do You Control The Attacks From Negative Fear?**

F   face your fears with honesty

E   examine your life from learning lessons

A   address your concerns immediately

R   refuse to run from your life

# HUMAN DICTIONARY
*The only definition your life has to truth is what you tell it.*

Stress is a fact! The sooner you realize that fact and address your life, the calmer your life will become. Most realize the fact of stress; they just don't deal with it while it can be controlled.

As I travel and teach people about how to live an abundant life, I find most don't want to face their life with honesty. Honesty that is presented that you don't want to hear makes for a very unpleasant situation.

I was speaking for the Ohio Real Estate Investors Association in Columbus on the subject of *Getting Yourself Organized.* I made the statement "disorganized people are dysfunctional people who live with behaviors that increase their stress. Stacks create stress."

I was in the hallway after my presentation and saw him standing in the corner staring at me. I knew he was waiting for the people I was talking to to leave. As they left, he made his way toward me.

"You really know how to get under people's skin don't you?"

"Well, as much as I don't intend to, when you present information people aren't ready to hear, that tends to be the result. Did I get to you?"

"I think that's an understatement. You not only got to me, BUT I found myself sitting there getting angry at you. I knew you were right in everything you were saying, but I didn't want to hear it. I wanted to get up and leave, but I couldn't. My mind was telling me I needed to hear this. You were telling me what I didn't want to hear. It's hard to listen

When the "old" you senses the "new" you is gaining control, it attacks with a vengeance.

to your life being exposed in front of 1500 people. I just knew everyone knew you were talking to me."

Truth is always a challenge to hear when you don't want to hear it. What do you think most do at that point?

- *Some justify their behavior;*
- *Some shut the conversation off;*
- *Others just deny what is being said;*
- *Still others have lived their lie long enough they have made it truth.*

The result of any of these is personal stress. The challenge of facing *what is* and *what isn't* is a constant creator of negative stress. The negative aspect of this is created by the inner war that takes place.

For years I have made the inner war between the "old" you and the "new" you a major theme of my presentations. Most know something is happening, but they can't put it into words. The reality is they are involved in a war between their "old" self and their "new" self.

The "old" self is that emotional aspect of their life that controls all that they are. This aspect of you doesn't want you to improve; this aspect doesn't want you to grow; this aspect of you wants you to stay the same and live as you have always lived. This "old" self will fight any insights, information or event that is designed for your life to grow. Growth is the "old" self's #1 enemy. The challenge you face is the years the "old" self has had controlling all that you are.

How many times have you started something designed to improve your life and walked away before you completed it? That is the battle between the "old" you and the "new" you. This battle is for control of your life. This battle is over who gets to design your life. This is not an every now and then

47

battle; it is an everyday battle.

The "new" you is constantly challenging the control of the "old" you. Each time your life gets excited by a possibility that is the "new" you challenging the "old" you. Each time your mind shows you another aspect of living that will take your life beyond where you are that is the "new" you at work challenging your living design. The "new" you only wants one thing for your life — improvement.

Now — if the "old" you is about sameness and the "new" you is about improvement, do you think the collision between the two can create any stress for you?

This battle is constantly pitting your mind and your emotions against each other; it is constantly creating collisions between *what can be* and *what is*. That is stress, and most of the time it is not positive stress. Why? This battle wears you out mentally and emotionally. It leaves you unprepared for life. It pits calmness against worry, clarity against doubt, confidence against uncertainty. How many times have you wrestled with these? How many times has the wrestling match left you mentally and emotionally worn out?

What you can't afford to miss is the fact *the winner gets control of your life*. What does that mean? It means all you see, all you hear and all you demonstrate through behavior is the result of which has gained control of your life. The longer you live with the "old" you having control the more negative stress you are going to have in your life. Each time the "new" you wins one of the battles you are given a ray of hope and that positive energy charges your life with positive energy. That energy is translated into positive action and that positive action creates a belief that you can move beyond where you are. These moments are what keep you going. The tragedy is most of these are short lived.

Learn this and learn it well. War is not about fighting battles. Fighting battles is the demonstration of the war. All wars are about someone winning and someone getting defeated. What happens when a person feels defeated? Does it affect their inner spirit? You bet it does! Do you think this feeling of defeat will affect their stress level? You bet it will. All battles are about gaining control; all battles are about destroying the inner spirit.

Let me show you how smart the "old" you is. The "old" you understands the personal power the "new" you winning creates. It also understands the devastation that occurs when the "new" you suffers a defeat.

So, what does the "old" you do? It will allow the "new" you to have a win. What does that feeling of winning do to your spirit? It lifts you up; it creates a surge of positive energy; it allows your mind to think creatively. It gives you hope, a new feeling of confidence and a sense you can move beyond those things you have been wrestling with.

When the "old" you senses the "new" you is psyched, it attacks with a vengeance. It uses every weapon it has to knock the "new" you down and out. The "old" you understands each time the "new" you has its spirit sucked out, it becomes more challenging for the "new" you to get back up. Over a period of time do you think that can hamper a person's belief system? Do you think over a period of years this can throw you into a negative behavioral living style?

How powerful is worry when it is given free reign in your life? How powerful is doubt when there is nothing to challenge it? How controlling is uncertainty when there is no inner confidence to fight its presence? How much negative stress is created when all you can see are the wrongs? How much negative stress is there when life only has one picture to stare at?

Betsy was one of those people who had been programmed with a negative picture of self. When she came to see me, her entire posture said, "I am not worthy."

During our first session together, I listened closely to see if I could hear any positive statements about her life. During our 90 minutes together, there were none. I listened as she described herself and was amazed at her self-perception. No wonder her life was upside down and driven by constant emotional pain.

At our second session I ask her, "Betsy, why do you see yourself as such a bad person?"

She paused, looked at me with hurt in her eyes and said, "That is all I have ever been told about me."

"Okay," I said. "Tell me what you have been told about yourself."

There was a long silence, and I knew this was a real tough time for her. Her lips quivered; her eyes swelled with tears; she slumped in her chair.

"I really don't want to talk about this."

"Betsy, if we don't work through this, you are going to be the way you are now the rest of your life. You came to me wanting to improve your life. You told me you were tired of the way things were. Do you want to get through this?"

"Yes! I guess I didn't realize what that meant."

"Okay, tell me what you have been taught about yourself."

"It's not my mom. She doesn't make me feel like a nobody. It is my dad. He is not nice to me. Anytime I talk to him he always reminds me of three things. He tells me I am ugly. So many times I have heard him ask my mother how we got such an ugly daughter."

You could feel the emotions that were tearing at her insides. She paused, reached for a Kleenex, wiped her eyes and continued. "My father would also remind me that I was stupid. Any idea I had was a dumb idea. He would ask me for my opinion and then rip it apart by telling me that was just plain stupid. I got to the place where I wouldn't answer his questions, but that didn't help. He would just make fun of my silence. Anytime I talked about what I wanted to do with my life, he would just laugh. He makes me feel so worthless."

I didn't see any of this in her. As I listened, I heard a very intelligent young lady, who with a little help with hair and makeup, could be very beautiful.

She was a living example of *the only definition your life has to truth is what you tell it.* Her father attacked her emotionally. Those emotional attacks created her opinion of herself. Since she had nowhere to go and no one to tell her any differently, his words created who she saw herself as. It took me almost a year to get her beyond what her dad had done to her life. It took her moving out and creating a life without his negative presence. I wish you could see her today. She is married, the mother of two beautiful daughters and an elementary school teacher.

Several years after she had repainted her picture of herself, she and I sat down for coffee in Tampa, Florida. My question to her was simply, "how are you doing?"

"I am doing great. It has not been easy getting to know this new person, but I like me. I'm not telling you there are not still times when that "old ugly" me comes calling. Certain things happen and I find myself slipping back into some of those old emotional struggles. I have to instantly stop and face the "old" me. I just don't ever want to be that way again. Thank you for being patient with me and for taking the time to help me through that old stuff. I am not sure I would have had that much patience."

"Betsy, it wasn't about patience. It was about your desire to get past your dad's programming. You don't know how many people there are like you out there."

She smiled and interrupted me. "Yes I do. I see them everyday. I listen as they have these ugly conversations about their life. They don't have anything good to say about who they are, where they are or what they are doing with their life. I want to shake them and tell them they don't have to live that way. I want to tell them that their words are not truth; they are only perceptions they have been programmed with. Richard, these people are so stressful. Their lives are so empty. I can't believe I ever allowed my dad to do that to me. I will never let anyone treat me that way again."

"Betsy, you are the exception, rather than the rule. For every one of you there is out there, there are a hundred that have never gotten beyond the negative program they have been handed. People need to hear your story. You need to take every opportunity with those who are trapped in the negative program and share with them your story. They need to see it really is possible to break free and live a life where you see the good in you."

Betsy really is the exception, rather than the rule. Everyday I listen to the behavior of people and watch them act out a negative script they have been programmed with. Everyday I hear them talk about what they would like their life to be, but live a life based on the beliefs they have been programmed with. *The only definition your life has of truth is what you tell it.* When all you know is what others have programmed you with, that is all you can be. When you only see the bad and the ugly in you, you will never be free to live. The result will be a life filled with negative stress that is always attacking your spirit and leaving you an empty shell, rather than a fulfilled person. You don't have to live that way. You can repaint the picture and release yourself from the negative script, from the negative stress.

## How Do You Release Yourself From That Negative Script?

R   refuse to talk bad about you
E   edit, don't try to erase the old tapes
L   look for positive help
E   eliminate those who put you down
A   always look for a positive lesson
S   start today being kind to yourself
E   experience and enjoy the "new" you

## RIGHT AND WRONG
*Life is not about asking questions; it is about learning to ask the right questions.*

Stress is *anything in life that makes you uptight.* That means everyday you are dealing with some aspect of stress. That means there is no escaping it. That means you either face it or you try to run away from it. You are a living example of the fact you cannot run from it. The more you try to run away from those stressful situations, the greater your stress becomes.

What's interesting is you know that. You know you cannot avoid stress, yet you will spend time and expend energy trying to avoid what you can't avoid. Think about that! Isn't that really insane? Why not just stop and face what is happening, find the solution and move forward without all the emotional damage. Don't you think you would be happier? Don't you think your life would be calmer? Don't you think that would relieve much of the negative stress from your life?

I had finished the program I was doing on stress and had made several of the above statements in my presentation. I was standing with a group talking about stress when he pushed his way through the people.

"You know the problem I have with people like you?" were his words to me.

I didn't get a chance to respond before he continued with his finger shaking in my face. "You come here, say your pretty words and then leave. You are like so many who make life sound so simple. You need to wake up and live in the real world. Life is hell. It is not easy; it is not simple and you live to have pain and you die to get rid of it."

I wish you could have felt the energy of the group

The difference between a right and wrong question is what direction does the answer take you.

that was standing there listening to him rage on. When he had finished, there was a silence as they watched to see if I would reach out and kill him.

I smiled, placed my hand on his shoulder and responded, "you know the challenge I have with people like you?"

I paused to see if he would respond. He didn't; he just stood there with this look of uncertainty on his face.

"The challenge I have with people like you is you don't want your life to improve. You enjoy the mess your life is in, so when you hear someone talk about simplifying your life, you reject the information. If you accept it, you have to take responsibility and know you are accountable. For those who emotionally react like you, it is much easier to just blame people or things than face yourself with truth and honesty."

I think you can guess that my words didn't make him too happy. His face turned red, the veins in his neck popped out and he was speechless. I don't think he expected my response. You knew he wanted to say something, but there was nothing to say that wouldn't get him in deeper trouble. He stood frozen for a moment and then turned and walked away while mumbling to himself.

Those who were standing there listening were in shock. The look on some of their faces was priceless. I thought to myself "this is a good time to help them learn a lesson."

I walked over, sat down and motioned for them to join me. After they were seated I said, "He is a prime example of a person who is in love with his misery. He doesn't have to live that way. He has chosen to reject those things that could help him improve and hold on to those things that keep his life upside down."

Peter raised his hand, so I paused and nodded to him. "Richard, is life really as simple as you present it?"

"Peter, life is as simple or as difficult as you want to make it. Don't ever forget life is really about knowledge and behavior. The two are not independent of each other. You have to have both. Knowledge without behavior leads to confusion and frustration. Behavior without knowledge doesn't allow life to make sense. You have to gather the knowledge and implement the right behavior. Now, that is not challenging if you really want to improve. Most talk about wanting to improve their life, but maintain the same behavior. The result is an increase in personal frustration, adding to their confusion and an increase in their personal stress."

I paused to make sure they were all grasping what I was saying. "Does that make sense to you?" The nods of agreement told me they were at least listening to what I was saying.

"I have found over the years of working with people that knowledge is not the issue. I live by the thought *you already know*. The gentleman who just left knows what he should do. He really isn't searching for information; he is looking for people to validate his wrong behavior. Remember what you have heard me say over and over? Three words."

Three of them raised their hands. "Okay, together tell me what those three words are."

"Behavior never lies," they said in unison.

"That's right. Behavior never lies. No matter what you tell yourself or others, the reality is you are the result of your behavior. The wrong behavior will always feed your confusion, expand your frustration and make sure your life is filled with negative stress. That is a choice; it doesn't happen by accident. A person chooses their pathway and either works to improve their life or works to keep their life upside down."

I paused again to make sure they were still there.

"Would you like to hear the deeper part of this?"

The nods told me it was okay to go on. "Everyone tells you to ask questions. They are right, but limited in what they are saying. It is not about asking questions; it is about learning to ask the right questions."

The look of puzzlement on some of their faces told me some weren't sure what I was talking about.

"Listen! Every situation contains right and wrong questions. If you ask the wrong question, you are going to get the wrong answer. If you ask the right question, you are going to get the right answer. It is not about simply asking questions; it is all about asking the right questions."

Alice raised her hand. I paused and nodded to her to talk. "I understand what you are saying. I have been one who has mastered the art of asking the wrong questions. I had always been told when you are confused or uncertain ask a question. So I would do that. Many times the answers I would get would just make me more confused."

"Alice, that is exactly what I am talking about. We have all been taught to ask questions, but very few of us have been taught the difference between asking right and wrong questions. Now, here is the difference between a right and a wrong question. A wrong question will always feed the confusion and leave you still uncertain about what is happening or what to do. A wrong question is not solution driven. It is confusion based. Does that make sense?

"Yes!" was the response. "Then," Randy jumped in. "What you are talking about is understanding what the intent of the question is."

"Randy, that is a good way of putting it. Many people ask for help, BUT they set you up by asking the wrong questions. When you react, remember — you can't respond to a wrong question; you can only react — you do so with the wrong answer which feeds the situation with wrong information. When you ask the right question, you move toward a solution. The right question is always looking for a pathway through the event or situation that won't make you have to come and wrestle with it again."

The change in their energy presence told me I needed to slow down for a moment and let them catch up.

"Hey, how many of you have things in your life you have been wrestling with for years?"

The majority of them raised their hand. "Okay, how many of you who raised your hand have told yourself and others you wanted to get beyond this?

Again, all who had raised their hand the first time raised their hand again. "How many of you have asked a question only to have the answer confuse you even more?" Almost all of them raised their hand.

"That is what I am talking about. The wrong question cannot give you resolution; it can only make sure you stay confused. Will that confusion create stress for you?"

Alice jumped back in with "You bet! That is where I have been. I am so tired of running in a circle dealing with the same issues over and over. That is tiring. In fact it is more than tiring; it is exhausting. I know it is the reason I live with many of the physical things I live with. I am wearing myself out dealing with the same crap. I ask questions, but I am asking the wrong questions."

"Bingo Alice! That is right on. The difference between

a right and wrong question is what direction the answer takes you toward. If it takes you to the situation with more confusion, it is the wrong question. If it doesn't point you toward a solution, it is the wrong question. Asking the right question means slowing down and not being driven by what you are feeling emotionally. Asking the right questions means letting your mind focus on getting through this. Your mind knows the right questions. Your mind knows what needs to be done, BUT because most are more emotional than they are logical, they tend to ignore their mind and listen to their emotions. Learn to ask the right questions and you learn to control your stress. Continue to ask the wrong questions and you increase your stress and sink deeper into an emotional gully that keeps life looking dark and impossible to understand."

Now, does this make sense to you? How many times have you fed your confusion by asking the wrong question? You felt you were right by asking the question, but you were wrong for asking the wrong question.

I really believe that life is simple. I really believe you don't have to live struggling with situations. I really believe you can move forward and not get trapped in the confusion of life. One of the keys is mastering the art of asking the right questions. That means slowing down emotionally and allowing your mind to frame the question. Your mind will always ask a question looking for clarity. Your mind will always be seeking direction through the event, not justifying staying in the event. The right question will expand your focus and grant you the spirit of hope. It will allow you to feel "I can get to the other side of this."

## How Do You Learn To Ask The Right Question?

R    refuse to accept confusion as an answer
I    investigate and find options
G    get a grip on your emotions
H    have a foundation of self-trust
T    the pace is everything

## KNOCK YOURSELF OUT

*When your mind and your emotions are at war, you will feel it mentally, emotionally, physically and spiritually.*

Stress is your friend or your enemy; the choice is yours. Stress is not something to take for granted; the result can be deadly. Stress is your emotions defining what is happening in your life. The sooner you understand that the easier it will be for you to control which aspect of stress you will deal with. Stress is a daily fact that affects every aspect of your life. It is present at work, at home, at play and when you are simply spending time alone with you. It is always present and everywhere in your life.

I met Barry through one of my private coaching students. He is in his mid 40's, successful, well educated, a workaholic, single and out of sync with life.

Now, you would think a person with all that going for them would be on top of their life. Barry could be, but a decision he made several months ago has his life lost in confusion.

Barry was just building his business when he met Victoria. She was a knockout. When Barry first saw her, he was captivated by her appearance. As he got to know her, he found that she was not only outwardly beautiful, but inwardly a person with the same level of beauty. WOW! That was what he had talked about wanting in a marriage partner. To top it all off she was successful in business, had a great personality and a brain she used.

Barry told me on one occasion, "The challenge I have with most women is that they are outwardly beautiful, but inwardly they don't have much upstairs."

As much as you would like to, you cannot rationalize emotions. The more you try the more stress and confusion you create for your life.

I know that is a sexest remark, but when you are only looking at the outside of a person you don't spend much time learning the other aspects of their personality. Barry was driven by the looks, and that was the reason most of his relationships didn't last very long. He had not met that one person who could steady his neck so he wasn't constantly comparing what he was looking at to what was walking by.

Victoria was different. She offered him a total package, and he hadn't experienced that before. Barry had one challenge. He was afraid of commitment. He had come from a home that hadn't done a good job of presenting a picture of a healthy relationship. His relationship with his father was not much; his relationship with his mother was good, but in some ways he had taken on the role of parent with her. There was so much missing in his understanding of love. Being a very analytical person, he tended to rationalize everything. If he couldn't rationalize it, he couldn't understand it.

This created one aspect of the confusion in his relationship with Victoria. She was a very touchy feely type of person who needed a lot of personal attention. Her home life was so different from Barry's. She came from a home that placed its emphasis on family, on love, on being together.

She wanted to spend time with Barry; he thought he needed to give the majority of his time to his business. After all he was just turning the corner in his business and it needed his undivided attention. As Barry told me, "If she had really loved me, she would have understood where my business was."

He forgot that Victoria's father had put family before business. His lack of understanding about love created a clash between what his emotions and mind were telling him. Rather than slowing down to understand what was happening, he just

increased his work pace. After all, love was an emotion and
Barry wasn't into spending time understanding his emotional
side. That would take time he needed to give his business.

Victoria wanted Barry to shut the business off when he
was with her. She told him she understood his business needs,
but at least when they were together, turn it off and spend the
time they did have with her.

This created another collision point for Barry. He knew
he needed to do that, BUT there was always a business crisis
he needed to take care of. When they were out, he would leave
his phone on. When they were supposed to be spending quality
time together, he was still in his business mode.

Finally, Victoria got tired of Barry's immaturity. She
ended the relationship, left New York and went back to the
west coast. Barry was devastated. He couldn't understand how
she could do that. In one conversation he posed this question to
me. "Richard, why couldn't she see how much I loved her?"

My response was, "Barry, put yourself in her shoes.
What if she was all business and each time you wanted to
spend time with her, she was present physically, but absent
emotionally. How would that have made you feel?"

"But my business needed me. I couldn't just let it run
its own course. I tried to tell her it wouldn't always be that way,
but at this time I had to give it all my energy. If she loved me,
she would understand."

"Barry, that sounds good, but it really doesn't fly. I
think the issues here are really two. First, you are trying to
rationalize something that can't be rationalized. Love is an
emotion, and you can't rationalize emotions. That is what you
have to understand. The second issue is I think you are afraid to
commit for the fear of being hurt. There is so much hurt in your

past you can't see beyond it. The fear controls you and won't allow you to be honest about how you feel about Victoria."

I paused to let him emotionally catch up. "Barry, I have a question for you. Are you in love with Victoria?"

The look on his face told me he was wrestling with the question. "I don't know if I am or not. How do you know if you are in love with someone?"

"Do you miss her when you are away from her? Does she have a constant presence in your mind? Do you find yourself longing to be with her? Do you want to be with her?"

"Yes to your questions, BUT how do you know if that is love?"

"Barry, there you go again. You are trying to rationalize something you can't rationalize. Love is not something you can rationalize. Every time you try to rationalize it, you are creating a battle between your mind and your emotions. That is a war you can't win, but you can lose."

The look on his face told me he didn't grasp that statement.

"Barry, the more you try to rationalize love the more confusing it will become. Love is something you have to experience by making yourself emotionally vulnerable. You have to let go of your fears and take the risk of emotionally exposing yourself. Does that make sense?"

"Yes, BUT it is not rational."

"Stop that! Love is not something you can rationalize. Do you miss her? Do you find yourself wanting to get on an airplane and go get her? Do you have this empty feeling inside you?"

"Yes, but what if she doesn't want me? What if I have permanently closed the door?"

67

"Now you are talking like a man who is in love with a woman."

Since the beginning of those conversations, Barry has been making moves to show Victoria how much he cares about her. He has rethought his life design and realized how much he is in love with her. Recently, she has come back to the City, and they have been spending time together.

Victoria told Barry, "The only way I would consider getting back together with you is if we are engaged."

Barry came to me confused with her words. "What is she saying? That I have to commit to marrying her to be with her. That isn't fair."

"Barry, you are not hearing what she is saying. Your mind and your emotions are so tangled up you have no clarity. Barry, she is simply sharing with you her confusion. She was in love with you and you weren't there. She was ready to get married, and your behavior stopped her in her tracks. She doesn't want to go through that again. Being engaged is her way of seeing if you are serious. She is speaking to you from her emotions. She is just as confused as you."

"What you're saying is she is remembering the hurt she experienced and is trying to make sure I don't hurt her again. Her way of protecting herself is being engaged."

"You got it! Both of you are in love with each other, BUT neither of you can get past the pain you each experienced in the past part of your relationship."

"Okay! What do I do? I don't want to lose her from my life, but I also don't want to invest energy into this relationship only to have her leave. How can I be sure she really wants me?"

"As much as you would like to have guarantees, there

are none in relationships. That is why you can't rationalize them. They are emotion centered and emotion driven. Relationships are mentally confusing. The more you try to understand them mentally the more confusing they seem. Barry, you just need to slow down and have fun with Victoria. You both need to relearn how to be together, reconnect at a level of fun and refocus on what you love about each other. Don't make everything intense. Let conversations evolve; don't press things because you are fearful of losing her. If your fear of losing her gets too strong, you will chase her out of your life. Just remember when your mind and your emotions are at war, you will feel it. Enjoy the relationship; don't analyze things to the point you play the *what if* game. That will only make everything more stressful."

If you would re-think our previous chapter for one second. We talked about asking the right questions. Every time you ask the wrong question you set yourself up for a collision. That collision will always be your mind and your emotions fighting for control. When that war is happening, you will feel it in other areas of your life.

Let's go back to Barry for a second. His words are exactly what I am talking about.

"Richard, I am so confused and scattered right now. I have not been here before and am not sure how to handle it. My emotions are sending me one message and my mind is sending me another. One minute I listen to my emotions and the next minute I am agreeing with my mind. The difficult part of this is I have always been a person who can figure anything out. I don't get stuck, but here I am. I am mentally and emotionally torn by this whole thing. A big part of me just wants to scream *screw this* and just run away."

69

"Is that what you really want to do?"

"Yes and no! I don't know what I want to do. I just know I am tired; I am confused; I am frustrated; I am out of my comfort zone. This is not me. I don't know this person I am right now."

"Barry, welcome to the war of life. Welcome to the confusion that occurs when your mind and your emotions cannot agree on what you should do."

"Will I get through this? Will I get back to living a life that I can figure out?"

"Yes! You can do that now if you will slow down and listen to your emotions and stop trying to rationalize everything you are feeling. Don't worry about what might happen; just slow down and share your feelings with Victoria. I promise you she is just as confused as you are. One of you needs to take the risk of putting your true feelings on the table. Show her your strength, show her your depth of commitment, express to her through your willingness to be open how much you love and want this relationship to work."

Can you identify with any of this? Your war may not be a relationship; it may be your job. It doesn't matter where the war is occurring. When your mind and emotions are at war, you are going to feel it in other areas of your life. The result will be a sense of confusion. The result will be a feeling of being lost. The result will be a huge feeling of uncertainty. All this is going to do is increase your negative stress.

To end this war you have to slow your life down and face what is happening with a sense of calmness that is looking for the clarity, which will lead you through the situation with your mind and emotions working together. It sounds more difficult than it is. Your confusion is happening because you are listening to your mind and your emotions at separate times. You have to take what you are feeling and find the connection points to what you are thinking. Those are the points where you can find agreement. Work from there; don't wrestle with what your mind doesn't understand about your emotions. You cannot rationalize emotions. You have to find where your mind and your emotions are in agreement and start at that point. Only then will you be able to find the peace treaty that will bring your mind and your emotions together with a common agenda.

Oh, by the way, Victoria and Barry did get married and today enjoy a great relationship.

## How Do You Get Your Mind And Emotions Together On A Common Journey?

C    confront honestly your confusion
O    open yourself to risking
M    must state your confusion to the person
M    manage the pace; don't run
O    organize your thoughts
N    negotiate a peace treaty

## RUN FASTER
*Increase your pace and you increase your stress.*


Stress is real! It is not one of those things some people experience and other people don't. It is an everyday fact of life. Remember, *if you are alive, you are living with stress.*

Have you ever noticed how most people deal with issues in their life? They know the issue is there; they understand the effect it can have on their life, BUT they choose to pretend it doesn't exist. How many times have you heard statements like this:

- *"Oh, it's no big deal."*
- *"This too shall pass."*
- *"I'm tough and can handle this."*
- *"I just choose to pretend it doesn't exist."*
- *"I'll get through this just like I've gotten through everything else."*
- *"If it was meant to be, it will be."*


These sound great, BUT they are simply statements designed to avoid what is happening. If you could only understand the damage this does to you mentally and emotionally. Avoiding issues doesn't resolve them. Avoiding issues only feeds the internal confusion you are wrestling with. The result is an increase in your negative stress.

Avoidance behavior is simply you running away from what you need to face. Most don't walk; they run. They speed up emotionally and push themselves to get through what they are struggling with. Then, they wonder why they are tired; why they can't seem to find any clarity in their life; why they seem to keep repeating the same stressful event over and over. The

Running faster doesn't resolve
anything; it is simply continuation
with more negative stress

answer is not what they want to hear. Everything you think you are running away from, you are actually running toward.

When I made that statement to Vanessa, she didn't want to hear it. "I'm not running. I just can't get through this."

"What's the difference?" was my response.

"You're playing games with me. You know the difference."

"Vanessa, I want you to tell me the difference between running away and not being able to get through this situation. Is this the first time you have faced this?"

"No, but that doesn't mean I am running away."

"What does it mean?"

"It means — I don't know what it means."

"It means you are not facing the situation. If you were facing it, you would be looking for a solution, rather than living with your justification. All I have heard from you are reasons and excuses for the sameness in your life. Remember what we talked about during our last visit? Resolving anything has four steps:

- face what is,
- redesign what has been,
- strengthen your good,
- reach out to others who can help you become better.

Do you remember that conversation?"

"Yes," she said with a sheepish look on her face. "I remember you mentioning it. Richard, I don't want to face this. There is too much pain inside me. Each time I think about it, talk about it or want to do anything it, it just increases my stress. It seems so much easier to just avoid dealing with it and let it run its course in my life."

"Vanessa, you have just used the right term when you said run. The reality is it will run its course in your life, BUT what you have to understand is the course has no ending. It will run and run and run. Each time you feel its presence in your life, you are going to speed up. Oh, you may think you are getting through it, but you are not. You are only doing more internal emotional damage to yourself. Please understand what is happening. When you think it is gone, it is not. It is only sitting in an emotional corner in your life waiting to run the course again. It will remain in your life until you resolve it. This is not about running faster; it is about slowing down and facing the situation with a mental presence designed to get beyond it. Does that make sense to you?"

"I think so."

"Those are interesting words. You either understand or you don't. This is what gets so many people in trouble. They won't admit when they don't understand, but need to understand. If you don't understand something, just say so. It doesn't mean you are dumb. It simply means the words haven't found a clarity point in your life."

I paused to let that much sink in. "Vanessa, when you are wrestling with life, you filter everything through your emotions. The information doesn't start in your mind; it starts in your emotions and has to work its way through all the emotions you are feeling. Those filters don't create clarity; they add to your confusion. Then, you find that internal war being fought."

"Okay! I don't understand what you are saying. Well, I do understand part of it, but why is it so difficult to slow down and just face it?"

"Fear! That's the answer pure and simple. It is all about the emotion of fear."

"How do you keep fear out of the situation. I was comfortable being married to Jeff. I thought we had a great life. I never anticipated he would find someone else. I never anticipated being on my own with three children. Don't you think most women would be fearful?"

"Yes, and I would worry about you if you weren't. The fear is not the issue; it is what you do with the fear. You can either face it or run from it. The natural thing for most is to run from it. They figure if they deny it, it will go away. It doesn't; it is simply made stronger by the avoidance behavior. The answer is in slowing down and facing the fact it is there. Once you face it, it takes on a different emotional presence in your life. Once you face it, you can start to redesign what it is doing to you; once you face it, you can start controlling it and get beyond the negative questions it is causing in your life. Once you face it, you will be amazed how many positive answers there are for you to see. It all starts with facing the fact your fear is real; it is filled with pain; it is challenging your beliefs about you. Once you face it, you can begin to move beyond it. It really does start with admitting it is real and affecting your life."

Do you have any idea how many Vanessas there are out there? Do you have any idea how many people spend each day of their life denying there is anything they need to deal with. As long as they are not honest with self, they are trapped in an ugly life that has only one direction. That direction is to wear them down and wear them out.

I watch so many choose to run, rather than face. Oh, they can and do justify it. They have their story down pat. They have told it so many times it has become their standard process of justification. What they don't want to hear is the emotional damage they are doing to self. What they don't understand is what it is stealing from their life.

You cannot experience happiness when you are running away from life's issues. Happiness is the result of slowing down, resolving and knowing you don't have to continue to repeat your emotional confusion and exhaustion. Learn this and learn it well. *The lack of happiness increases the negative stress in your life.*

You cannot experience personal fulfillment when you are running from life's issues. Personal fulfillment is the result of feeling completed by what you have chosen to do with your life. That completion is in any aspect of your life. It is an inner excitement that allows you to see each day as an opportunity to stretch yourself and find the improvement that makes your life even better. Now learn this and learn it well. *The lack of personal fulfillment in your life will increase your negative stress.*

You cannot experience freedom when you are running from life's issues. The faster you run the further you get from the solution. The faster you run the more you become a prisoner to the situation. Freedom is about release. It is about being pardoned from any emotional situation that locks you behind a wall of fear. To get out of your emotional jail you have to slow down and start with facing what is.

Running faster is not an answer; it is simply continuation. Running faster makes sure your negative stress gains more emotional control.

## How Do You Learn To Slow Down?

S    stay focused on resolving the issue
L    lay your fears on the table
O    openly confront your fears
W   work through, not around issues

## Public Enemy #1
*Negative behavior creates negative stress.*

She asked if we could have breakfast together. I knew from the sound of her voice on the phone something was wrong. I was at the restaurant when she arrived. As she walked toward me, I felt this strange feeling come over me. She sat down, took a deep breath and just stared at me.

"You don't look too good. What's wrong?"

"Everything! Everything is wrong. I have really allowed myself to get trapped. Richard, not in just one part of my life, but in every part. I can't look at any room of my life without seeing a total emotional mess. Most days I just want to crawl into a corner and hide."

I knew by the look in her eyes she was very serious. Sherry had walked into my life six years prior and had been in and out of my life as her life went through different events. I hadn't seen or heard from her in over a year.

Sherry was one of these people who was her own worst enemy. She was intelligent, but didn't apply her smarts. She had become accustomed to people bailing her out. She had such a captivating personality people just wanted to take care of her. She always knew when her life got upside down, there would be someone who would bail her out. She had grown to depend on that.

The challenge with that behavior is after a while those who have constantly bailed her out get tired of being used. She would come to them with her upside down life; they would bail her out; then, she would disappear until the next time she needed them.

In the past I had talked to her about that behavior and

People stop listening to what
you say when your behavior is
saying something different.

explained to her the danger of using people, not appreciating people. She would say, "I know," but go right on with her behavior. Now, it had finally caught up to her.

"Okay Sherry, tell me what is going on."

"Are you sure you want to know? No one else has wanted to listen to me. It seems when you need people the most, they just disappear."

"Sherry, you and I have talked about your behavior of using people. We have talked about the fact a time would come when they would get tired of you running to them for help, using their kindness and then, throwing them aside until your next crisis. People don't like to be treated that way. People get tired of giving when they feel they are being used. Reality is Sherry — you are good at using people for your own need. That negative behavior makes people not want to be around you. Now, to answer your question. Yes, I would like to hear what is going on in your life. Tell me."

"You don't pull any punches, do you?"

"No! When you don't shoot straight with people, you give them permission to stay the same. Playing games with people is a waste of everyone's time and energy. Help can only be found when you have people in your life who confront your behavior, refuse to adopt you and force you to be accountable for your behavior. Sherry, the reason you are still living in this negative behavioral circle you have created for your life is the fact people step up and take care of you; they don't step up and make you accountable. I will not participate in your crisis, but I will listen and see if I can guide you through the mess you have gotten your life into. Now, do you still want to share with me what is happening in your life?"

"That is one of the things I hate about you. You don't

cut me any slack. As much as I hate you, I also respect you for doing that. Richard, I have really messed up this time. I have lost my job, allowed my finances to get out of control and pushed away the only person who really cared for me. I guess you could say I have taken strike three."

"Sounds like you have really turned your life upside down and inside out. Okay, let's take this one step at a time. Tell me about losing your job."

"You know I am not a morning person. The hardest thing for me is to get up in the morning. I had been constantly late for work. The boss I had understood me and told me as long as I made up the time, I could come in a few minutes late. Well, she got promoted into a different department and they replaced her with this witch. This lady was not nice. She was rigid and wouldn't compromise for anyone. She told me I had to be on time. Richard, I tried, but I am not a morning person. I was late several times and because of that, she let me go. I tried talking to her and she just let me know I had used up all my chances."

"Sounds like you met another person who held you accountable for your behavior. Did your job require you to be there at a specific time?"

"Yes! I was to be there at eight."

"What time were you showing up?"

"It wasn't too bad. I was always there by 8:30 to 8:45."

"You don't consider that bad?"

" Well, I showed up and when I was there I worked. That is more than I can say for some of the other people who were there. They would get there on time, but not work. At least when I was there I worked."

"And because you worked while you were there, she

should excuse your tardiness?"

"Well, I did my job!"

"Sherry, it is great you did your job, but you wanted to play by your own set of rules. Any manager understands you can't allow a person to do that. If she allowed you to do that, she would have to allow everyone to come and go as they pleased. How many times did she talk to you about being late?"

"I don't know. Maybe five."

"She had five conversations with you and you didn't get the message? I am not sure I would have been that patient with you. How long ago did you lose your job?"

"Four months ago."

"What have you been doing for the past four months?"

"Well, I have been thinking about my life. I have been trying to figure out what I want to do."

"That sounds like an excuse to me. Have you been looking for a job?"

"No! I don't know what I want to do."

"How have you been living?"

"Jerry has given me some money. He told me I could pay him back when I got a job."

"Okay, what has happened with Jerry?"

"He left me. He told me he was tired of being involved with a child. He told me I needed to grow up. I don't understand why he left. I was good to him. We had been dating for a little over a year. I was there for him, and then, when I needed him, he just walked away. I guess he didn't care as much as I thought he did."

"Wait a minute! I'm thinking you are missing what has happened here. He got tired of your behavior. He got tired of listening to your stories that never happened. Sherry, sounds

like he decided you needed to be accountable for your life.
How much money are we talking about and how long did you
owe it to him?"

"It was a few thousand dollars. He loaned it to me right
after I lost my job. I would have paid him back."

"Had he loaned you money before?"

"Yes, but that was different."

"Different? How was that different?"

"He didn't expect me to pay it back."

"How do you know that?"

"Well, he never mentioned anything about paying it
back. I had told him I would, but he never made a big deal out
of it."

"Sherry, you are a mess. People don't give you
money, just to give you money. They loan it to you. Do you
understand the word 'loan!' They don't give it to you without
the expectation you are going to pay it back. Most people are
not made of money and don't have money to just throw away.
Jerry had a right to get upset with you. You said you lost your
job over four months ago and hadn't really been trying to find
anything. You were trying to figure out what you want to do
when you grow up. I think the message people are sending
you is GROW UP! People don't walk away because they don't
care; they walk away because they get tired of what they are
experiencing. If you stopped and looked at your behavior, you
have sent a very negative message. You have told people they
are simply there to take care of you. People get tired of that.
Does this make sense to you?"

"I guess so."

"You guess so! It either makes sense to you or it
doesn't. Does this make sense to you?"

"Okay; it makes sense to me. BUT why did they all have to leave right now. My life is more upside down now than it has ever been. I don't think I can handle much more stress in my life. The pressure is making me physically ill. I just need to get out of this mess."

Her words were correct. She needed to get out of the mess she had created for herself. Yet, Sherry is like so many. They get their life upside down, scream wolf and expect everyone to come running. People will do that for a while, but soon the behavior makes them close their ears when they hear the cry.

Sherry, like so many, needed to be accountable for her behavior. She needed to understand *negative behavior creates negative stress*. It is important you understand that all behavior is fed by emotions and in turn all behavior feeds behavior. The behavior you see in people is a statement about who they see themselves as. All behavior has an affect on a person spiritually, mentally, emotionally and physically. If the behavior is negative, the affect is going to be negative; if the behavior is positive, the affect is going to be positive.

Until they realize this, they will always be on a collision course with self and with those who are part of their life. Negative behavior sends a negative message to those who are part of their life. Over a period of time people grow tired of feeling used.
As much as they may care, at some point they will have had enough. When they reach that point, they will walk away. Most won't tell you why they are leaving; they will simply leave.

Your enemy is your behavior. What people see you as, think you are or understand you to be, is all defined by your behavior. When the behavior is negative, they soon paint a negative picture of you. The wear and tear on them increases their stress, and when it is enough, they will walk away.

## How Do You Control Negative Behavior?

N    never lie to yourself about your behavior
E    emotionally face yourself
G    get help if you can't help yourself
A    accountability is a big key
T    talk out loud to yourself
I     increase your personal time
V    victim mentality is not acceptable
E    eliminate all that feeds this behavior

## JUST PLAIN UGLY!
*Anger takes stress to the danger zone.*

Stress is a fact! I hope you understand that by now. It is not something to take lightly in your life. It is like all emotions. It has a good and a bad side. What aspect of this emotion you have in your life is your choice. You can't blame situations or events for what is happening. The result of any situation is in your hands. If you choose to make it a growth event, you can do that. If you choose to let it tear your life down, you can also do that.

Of all the emotions that you will deal with in your life anger is one of the most dangerous. Anger is a time bomb that just sits inside you waiting to find a reason to explode. When it does, the ripple effect is devastating for everyone who is in the path of the outburst.

Understand what I am about to say. I like people who have a temper. Does that sound strange? Too many see temper and anger as the same. They are not. Let me see if I can help you see the difference.

Temper is an emotion created by an event and expressed at the level of heightened concern. Now, catch the words here. It is an emotion. It is an expression of what you are feeling and is designed to try to bring resolution and clarity to an event where the participants may not be listening.

How many times have you had someone tell you they were listening and you knew they weren't? They were just telling you that to get you to shut up. To get them to listen you had to change your personal presentation in order for them to understand how serious you were. Yes, you were upset. Yes, you may have raised your voice, but your agenda was to get

89

Anger is always present, but
is not always visible.

them to work with you to resolve what was happening.

This behavior is not destructive. Others may not enjoy it, but the expression of temper is not destructive. As long as the agenda is resolution and clarity, it has a positive framing.

Anger is a different story. It is not about resolving anything. It is not about seeking clarity. The agenda of anger is to seek and destroy. Anger is one of the emotions I classify as ugly. It seeks to hit you at the center of your spirit. It will use any and all weapons at its disposal to do its ugly damage. It not only wants to hurt the other person; it wants to destroy them from the inside out.

Here are two important aspects of anger you must understand. First, *anger is always present, but not always visible.* Anger does not come and go. Anger has a constant presence. Just because you don't always see it, doesn't mean it is not there. Anger is always present.

The second thing you need to understand is *anger is triggered by a connection.* Many times the person who is the blunt of the outburst is not the cause of the anger. Anger is an emotion that hides inside you, and when something happens, the event has an emotional connection to the trigger and is set in place. The event triggers the anger which races backward to the foundation event and that causes the explosion. Whoever is present when the trigger is squeezed will get the full force of the anger.

That triggering can be set off by the use of a word, a situation, a picture or a number of other things. The challenge is knowing what the trigger is for the person. The controlling of the anger demands finding the foundation for the anger and redesigning it.

Finding that foundation is a journey that demands a

lot of time and patience. I have found many who have lived with this anger cannot pinpoint its origin. Many times in the counseling room what you think is the foundation is not. Many who live with this ugly emotion cannot remember the event that has caused the festering. It is buried so deep in their subconscious it takes a lot of psychological searching to discover it. Why is it so challenging to find it? Most of the time the pain and scaring was so great the person has buried it deep within their inner being. When the anger erupts, they can't control the outburst. It is like an inner fire that can't be contained. They can work to contain it, but it is going to get out.

This makes anger one of the most powerful of all emotions. It is right up there with fear. These two I believe are the most self-destructive emotions you will ever deal with.

I met Billy at a program I was doing. The gentleman who had hired me sent him out to talk to me.

On the surface Billy was the nicest person you would ever meet. Here was this 6'2" giant with hands that rapped around mine telling me he had a real problem with anger. The smile, the gentleness with which he presented himself seemed to contradict all that he was saying. Yet, the look in his eyes told me he was serious about his challenge with anger.

I knew we didn't have the time nor was this the place to really discuss his situation, so I arranged to meet with him the next week. As fate would have it, I was going to be in his city speaking and had a free morning we could spend together.

As we sat down for breakfast, his opening words caught my attention.

"Richard, last week I came within an inch of killing myself. I was driving down this two-lane highway and had

this semi coming toward me. This little voice inside me kept
screaming at me *turn the wheel; pull in front of it; your life
isn't worth anything; get out of your misery; go ahead do it; do
it!* I was that close to just turning the wheel and running head
on into the truck."

"What stopped you?"

"In the same instance I saw the faces of my three
daughters, and I couldn't do that to them. It's like I have this
fire raging inside of me. I can't control it. At times I can get
away from it, but it doesn't take much for it to turn into a
raging fire I take out on everyone around me."

"During the day when you are calling on customers,
does it come out?"

"Not when I am in front of them. I push it down and
do the smiling thing. BUT when I get in the car, I just want to
run over people. The worst is when I get home. I feel sorry for
Jada. She gets it all thrown at her. I walk in and immediately
start looking for something to scream at her about. The kids
come running to me and I don't want to be around them. Know
what?"

"What?"

"I just want to get in my car and drive away. I want to
run away and hide where no one can find me. I am so tired of
living with this rage inside of me. It is slowly killing me and
those around me."

"Billy, can you tell when this rage is about to happen?"

"Sometimes I can feel it coming. Those are the times
when I try to get away from people. I know I am going to hurt
them in some way. Other times it sneaks up on me. My day can
be going great, and then out of nowhere, this rage just comes
sweeping over me. As much as I try to push it down, I can't. I

am so tired of living this way. There are days I think death is the only way out."

"Is there any one thing that seems to trigger your anger? I mean when it happens, is there any consistent event happening?"

"My doctor asks me the same thing. I don't think so. I have thought about that and it just seems to come from left field. I just want it to stop; I just want it to go away. I can't continue to live this way. The stress I put on me and others is ugly."

There was this long pause while he gathered himself emotionally. It was challenging sitting there and watching this giant of a man wrestle with this ugly emotion that had invaded his being and was breaking him down.

"Sunday I really lost it. I was so ugly with Jada. She finally told me she couldn't take it anymore. She told me I was destroying her and emotionally tearing the kids apart. She said she thought it would be best if I just moved out. I know I have hurt her. I know my anger has really damaged our relationship. I know my anger is affecting our kids. I watch my middle daughter act just like me. She has my personality, and I can see myself in her behavior. That hurts and scares me. I couldn't live with myself if she became like me. They all might be better if I wasn't there."

There are so many people like Billy. They live with this inner fire; they live not liking what it does to them, but not knowing what to do about it. Many control it with medication. I am not saying that is bad, but it is not a cure. The medication is only a stopgap. The only cure is finding the inner event that sparked the fire. That means a commitment of time; that means some very deep emotional searching; that means uncovering things that have been emotionally buried deep inside the person. This demands a patient presence from all involved.

The person wrestling with the anger must understand and accept this is not an overnight journey. It will demand a commitment of time and an openness to examine all areas of their life.

It will also demand a patient presence from those who are involved in this person's life. Many times this person's inner circle of people gets the blunt of the anger. Like Billy, many don't react to their environments outside their inner circle; the events outside the inner circle spark the inner rage, but those in their inner circle feel the heat of the fire. On more than one occasion Jada told me about her desire to run away from Billy. She was tired of "the crap" he kept throwing at her and the kids. She was on the edge of having had Enough! After several conversations she realized the anger was not about her; she was the outlet for the anger. That didn't take away the hurt and damage Billy's anger did to her, but it did give her an insight into what was happening. She loved Billy enough she was willing to help him work through his ugly presence. That meant a lot of patience; it meant a lot of understanding; it meant slowing down and sensing what was happening in Billy's life.

Anger really is an ugly emotion. Let me go back to how we began this discussion. All behavior has an agenda. There is no positive side to anger. It only has one agenda and that agenda is destruction of another person's spirit.

It is important you remember there is more than one person who lives inside of all of us. Each has an ugly, a negative, a positive and an ultimate aspect to their personality. The aspect that is predominant guides your life. Given the right situation, the ugly aspect of your personality can get lose. When and if that happens, you become dangerous to yourself and others.

The ugly aspect is the only part of you that is really dangerous. Yes, the negative is not pretty, but the negative is a pussy cat compared to your ugly side.

The negative aspect of your personality really is seeking attention. It has learned "if I am bad, I get attention." So, it creates negative situations so it can be noticed.

No so with your ugly side. This aspect of your personality doesn't care about being noticed. That is the last thing on its agenda. The ugly wants to inflict pain that will be remembered. It wants to drive an emotional stake through the essence of your soul. It is driven by an anger that doesn't care what you think about it. It just wants to inflict such pain that you will be emotionally wounded and scared. This is why it is so challenging to forget those whose ugly side has been part of your life.

This ugly aspect of your personality doesn't have just one face. It has several faces and the degree of the inner fire determines which face of anger you see. Anger can go from spiteful to mean to attacking to destructive.

I remember one conversation with Jada and Billy where we were talking about Billy playing Candy Land with the kids. Jada looked at Billy and said to me. "He can't even play a game with the kids. If he is losing, he gets angry. I have seen him scream at the kids and throw the game board across the room. It scared the kids and they ran to their room crying. Tell me that isn't abnormal?"

When Billy's ugly side was running wild, he would do things he knew would upset Jada. In one conversation we talked about an event where he came home to a house that was tension filled. Jada had had the three kids all day long and two of them had been sick. When Billy walked in, Jada asked if he would take the kids and play with them while she finished getting dinner ready.

Jada said, "He looked at me with this evil smile, turned, walked into his study and closed the door. He knew it would make me angry, BUT he just didn't care."

"Billy," I said. "Did you mean to upset Jada?"

"I just had had one of those days, and I didn't want to be around the kids."

"Didn't you sense that Jada needed your help? Didn't the sound of her voice seem like a cry for help to you?"

"I guess so, but I just didn't want to be around the kids."

"Billy, I think it was more than that. I think the ugly side of you was out, and you were being spiteful to Jada. You know her well enough to sense what type of day she has had. This was a way of getting to her. Could that be an accurate statement?"

There was this long pause while Billy stared at Jada. "Yes! I think that is an accurate statement."

"Billy, do you sense when you are doing these things that will upset and hurt her?"

"I know when I am doing them, but I just can't seem to stop. Inside there is this little voice that says *you know this is wrong*. As hard as I try, I can't stop what I am doing. After, I feel so sorry, but I know if I say *I'm sorry*, it will mean nothing to her. I have just done it too many times before."

Anger, in any form, takes a person to the place of loss of control. In all the people I have worked with who had an anger problem they knew what they were doing, but couldn't stop it. Many have talked about wanting to stop the action, but it was like they were inwardly locked in a cell watching this person they didn't like take control of their body. Some talked about inwardly screaming at this emotional evader and not being able to stop what that ugly person was doing to someone they really loved.

When I would talk to the controlled Billy, I would ask him "Do you love Jada?"

The answer would come back, "At times."

"Richard, when I am not in my ugly state, I care very much for her. When this creature inside me is loose, I only want to hurt her. I know I would never physically hurt her or the children."

"Billy, can you be sure of that?"

"I think so. I mean I always have. I have never physically done anything to hurt her or the kids. I don't know what I would ever do if I lost it to that point. I couldn't live with myself if I physically hurt them."

The challenge with many is their anger crosses the line from inflicting emotional pain to inflicting physical pain. Anger has that power. Again, it is the trigger.

I worked with Chris for over a year. His ugly side was so dangerous we gave him a name — Chucky. You didn't want to be around when Chucky was loose. Chris was a giant of a man with tremendous physical strength. When Chucky was lose, Chris' physical strength increased. Research tells us anger increases physical strength. Chucky could punch a hole in a wall; he could tear a door off the hinges; he could knock a person out cold with one punch. I saw all three while working with Chris. My concern was who was I going to talk to — Chris or Chucky.

What we learned was Chucky was set free when Chris would drink alcohol. It only took about two drinks for Chucky to come out of his room and take over Chris' presence. As long as Chris didn't drink, Chucky was put away.

The ugly side of anyone is triggered by something. It can come in many forms, but when the trigger is in place, the ugly side is loose. When the ugly side is loose, the person is dangerous.

I need to remind you *the anger is always present, but not always visible*. When the anger is controlled, the person can be the nicest person you will ever meet. BUT -- let the ugly person come out and you would swear the person's body had been invaded by a foreign creature.

This behavioral inconsistency is what keeps those who are in the angry person's life hanging around. The challenge is they live in fear of coming face to face with the ugly monster. Their hope is the ugly monster will go away. It does for a while, and then returns with a vengeance.

Anger is a damaging emotion. Its agenda is to hurt others, but in the process it does emotional damage to self. Anger wears you out from the inside. It attacks everything good about you. It makes you not like you. When you stop liking you, you give your anger more control. It makes you want to run away. When you are running, you aren't facing what is happening in your life. That feeds the anger and gives it more control. The more control anger has in your life the more often you are going to find your ugly side alive and running rampant through your emotional life.

Anger is an emotion you can't handle by yourself. I have had several tell me, "I know I have an anger issue, but I can handle it." The truth is *you cannot handle it by yourself!* If you could, you would be on the other side of this ugly emotion and in control of your emotional presence.

Anger is an emotion you can't handle by yourself. To understand it you need someone who can guide you to discovering the emotional mine field that is triggering the explosions. That has to be discovered and diffused before the anger will ever be controlled. Medicine can help you control the explosions, BUT it cannot solve the anger.

You have to be willing to reach out and find someone who can guide you, not give you answers. You need an emotional guide that can walk you backwards until you find the trigger event. Only then, will you ever be free from the control this ugly emotion has over your life.

Now, don't try to fool yourself. There is nothing pretty about anger. It is the ugliest of all your emotions. Just because it comes and goes does not mean it is not always present. Firefighters will tell you even if you can't see the flames of a fire doesn't mean there aren't embers burning under the surface. The same is true with anger. This is your worst enemy. Remember what you were taught as a child -- don't play with fire. You will get burnt! Don't play with anger; it will consume your life.

**How Do You Start Controlling Your Anger?**

A   admit you have an issue with anger
N   never pretend it was an accident
G   get honest about this being an issue
E   exit when you feel the fire exploding
R   reach out for qualified help

## WHO ME WORRY?

*Worry, for the most part, is an emotion that creates tension where it is not necessary.*

Stress can be dangerous, BUT it doesn't have to be. Stress is a fact of life, BUT it does not have to be a negative part of living. The more you understand that stress is an emotional attachment the easier it will be for you to control the negative attachments it has on your life. One of those attachments is the emotional reaction we call worry.

Do you ever worry? Do you ever worry about things you can't control? Do you ever worry about things you could control, but just don't want to face? Does worry ever exhaust you? How many times have you worried about something, it finally happens and it isn't near as bad as you worried it would be?

For the most part worry is a nonsense emotion. It is the investment of your energy in an event or situation that you are either uncertain about, fearful of, confused with, frustrated by or just not wanting to face. Any or all of these are emotionally draining. The result will be an increase in your negative stress.

As much as you may not want to hear this, *worry is one of the negative emotions created by your desire to avoid.* Does that make sense to you?

I have found most who get caught up in the game of worry are seeking an excuse or a way to avoid facing the issue. Worry gives them a reason to procrastinate; worry gives them a justification for not facing what is; worry creates the reason they don't respond. None of these are positive; none of these resolve issues and free you from worry; none of these will do anything to reduce the stress in your life. The fact is many use

The fact is many use worry
as their excuse to avoid facing
the issues of their life.

worry as their excuse to avoid facing the issues in their life.
How many times have you heard a statement that
sounds like this:
- *I'm just worried sick about this.*
- *I'm too worried to do anything.*
- *There is too much worry to deal with this right now.*
- *I need to get through this before I do anything.*

Study these! None of them are designed to resolve the
issue or situation your life is facing. All are designed to give
your life permission to avoid dealing with what is.

Jack's opening words to me were, "I don't know how
to do anything but worry. I think it is a family trait I inherited
from my mother. The thing I remember most about her is her
chronic worrying. There was nothing she did not worry about."

Have you ever met someone and knew what was
happening in their life just by their physical behavior? That
was Jack. He was a walking, talking bundle of worry.

"I'm so tired of living this way. Richard, I have got
to get over the control worry has over my life. I get up in the
morning and immediately start worrying about what is going to
happen that day. I worry about whether I am wearing the right
clothes, eating the right breakfast, whether the traffic is going
to make me late, and that's just the start of my day. This pattern
continues through my entire day. Maybe I am just crazy."

"Jack, you are not crazy. You are just consumed by
playing the *what if* game."

The look on his face told me he wasn't real sure what I
was talking about.

"Jack, chronic worriers always play the *what if* game. In
their mind they create these scenarios about all the things that

might happen, might go wrong or could be. As they are doing this, they are emotionally working their self into a frenzy. The worry takes over their emotional sight, and they can't see anything with emotional clarity. This game just wears them out."

"I know that feeling. I am so tired at the end of each day. I come home and I am useless to myself or my family. All I want to do is go to bed. My wife told me it is getting harder and harder to put up with my behavior. I know she is right. I bark at her and the kids, and if I am not barking, I am just silent. Either punishes them. All that does is give me something else to worry about. God knows I don't need that."

Granted, Jack is an extreme case, but he illustrates the power worry can have over a human life. Worry is a draining emotion. There are some emotions that replenish the energy they take out of you, and there are others that take and don't replenish. Worry is one that takes and doesn't replenish. Without the replenishing the worry leaves you weaker and weaker. The more you work to control it, the bigger the *what if* game becomes. That means more stress.

The key is not to work to stop worrying, but to learn to control the arenas where the worry is happening. You will never stop worrying. It is a part of life that will always be, but it doesn't have to have a negative effect on your life.

To learn to control your worry you must understand where your worry comes from. Over the years I have found some common pathways that worry uses to slip into and take control of your life.

The first of these is the *what if* game. This is a very dangerous game. It takes you to the world of the unknown and poses a situation designed to ask a negative question. Some would say "asking *what if* is not negative; it is preventive medicine. It is allowing yourself to be prepared if the worst should happen."

The challenge with that is you are allowing your emotions to think about the worst, rather than believing the best can happen. The worst will always feed your worry and send you into an emotional state of reacting.

How many times have you seen people play the *what if* game? How many times have you heard things like:
- *What if I get really sick?*
- *What if I lose my job?*
- *What if I get into a car wreck?*

None of these are positive questions; the *what if* game is simply a way of creating worry for yourself. That means you are not thinking solution; you are thinking problem.

Worry also comes from *opinions not being supported by facts*. This is another dangerous game. It replaces *I know* with *I feel*. When your life is designed around what you feel and your feeling is based on precluding the worse, you become a danger to yourself.

How many times have you heard statements like this:
- *I feel I am going to lose my job.*
- *I feel my wife is going to leave me.*
- *I feel I have cancer.*
- *I feel he doesn't like me anymore.*

None of these are designed to resolve; each is designed to sink you deeper into your personal pit of worry. Without information you are playing a dangerous emotional game each time you are guided by *what you feel*, not *what you know*.

105

Worry can also come from *refusing to let go of yesterday*. The pains and frustrations of yesterday only repeat themselves in today because you drag them into your present. When yesterday becomes a nagging part of today, today will become stressful before it arrives. That means the things you worried about yesterday have a continuation in today. That is a dangerous emotional game. It sets you up for a series of expectations you will make happen.

How many times have you heard statements like:

- *This is just going to be a repeat of the last relationship I had.*
- *My life is just one giant circle of problems.*
- *This is the way it has always been.*
- *I am just like my mother.*

None of these are designed to allow you to see the pathway to improvements. Each is designed to take you down the same road of frustrations you have been traveling. Again, it just becomes more manna for your worry.

Another common pathway for worry is *reacting to what you can't control*. At some point in your life you have heard someone say "deal with the things you can control and let go of those things you can't." That is good advice, but really challenging for most to do.

It is so easy to want to jump in and take control of things you don't have any control over. It is so challenging for most to stay out of things and places they shouldn't be involved in. There is something interesting about people who are chronic worriers; they love to seek out things to worry about. I mean, even if those things have nothing to do with them, they want to jump in and give their two cents worth. They are always talking about what they would do "if" they were in charge. Again, this is just more manna for their emotions to feed on, and the result is an increase in their worry.

The last common pathway I have seen worry travel is *your continual searching for the catastrophes.* This is the strongest characteristic of the chronic worrier. They aren't happy if there is not a problem; they are sad if there is nothing for them to complain about. They are always searching and finding a catastrophe. What's interesting is they will always find one.

Have you ever known someone whose life was running smoothly and they said something like "something is wrong, really wrong. My life is going along too calm. Something bad is about to happen. I can just feel it."

This is a life that doesn't know what to do without something to worry about. They seek it, find it and then complain about all the problems in their life. They are their own enemy and will exhaust all the lives they are involved in. They make worry an acceptable part of life and fight anyone who seeks to remove it from their life.

Worry, when it is controlling your life, is a useless emotion. It attacks your life with doubt, skepticism and feeds your fear. It clouds you mentally and emotionally, while making you stare at all the perceived wrongs. It speeds your emotional presence and moves you to a world of reacting. Put all this together and what do you think it will do to your stress level? Anything that takes you away from having control of your life increases your negative stress. That means worry is creating tension in areas where it doesn't have to be. The result is a life that is worn down and filled with confusion and a sense of frustration and incomplete events.

**How Do You Control Your Worry?**

W work on improving relaxation skills
O openly talk to yourself
R recognize the limits of your control
R reach out to one who can help you
Y you must slow the pace down

# I'LL DO IT TOMORROW
*Procrastination is not a behavior that creates freedom;
it is a hostage taker.*

Negative stress is a result of negative and positive emotions colliding. You know what you should do, but talk yourself out of doing it. That means your mind and your emotions have different agendas, which pit them against each other.

The result is confusion. Confusion then becomes manna for your negative emotions to feed on.

The result is emotional tiredness. The result is the lack of energy to handle the issues you are facing.

Put confusion and the lack of energy together and you create a behavior called procrastination. Procrastination is one of those behaviors that punishes everyone involved in its presence.

I have met a lot of procrastinators in my time, but none more pronounced than Jackie. If there were a degree in Procrastination, she would have had her Ph.D.

I was speaking for a Real Estate Investors Conference in Columbus, Ohio when she and her husband Darren entered my life.

I was packing up my equipment when I heard this voice say, "How would you like a real challenge?"

I turned and there they were. Standing there with a look that said, "We dare you!"

"I'm always up for a good challenge. What are we talking about here?"

"Well," Darren said. "You were talking about disorganization and procrastination in your presentation today,

109

Procrastination is the
behavior of avoidance
justified through reasons,
excuses and blame.

and I think my wife might be a great piece of research for you."

She reached over and punched him on the arm as she said, "Darren! That's not nice."

Looking at her with question marks in his eyes, he said, "Well, am I wrong? Don't you proclaim to be the world's worst procrastinator?"

"Yes, but you know I am just joking."

"You may say it in jest, but you procrastinate with everything. Nothing gets your attention in a timely fashion. Your life is nothing but a bundle of confusion that I get sucked into."

"I don't think I'm that bad."

I just stood there and listened as the two of them had their own little private conversation. Finally, when there was a break, I asked, "How can I help?"

Without hesitation he looked me squarely in the eyes and said, "Work with her. I don't care what it costs. Work with her before she destroys all of our lives. Her confusion wears on everyone in and around our lives. Her procrastination keeps people from wanting to be around her. Every time they are there, they get sucked into her lack of completing things. Please, take her on as one of your students and get her through this. I am not asking; I am begging you."

I agreed to visit them in order to gather a picture of what he was talking about. I thought to myself, "It can't be as bad as he is painting it to be."

Boy was I wrong! I've seen homes that were messy, BUT never one where there wasn't a corner or a spot without a stack being there. The stacks were on the floor, on furniture, pinned to the wall and stacked on top of stacks.

Darren was watching my eyes as I was walking through

111

the house. He could see the disbelief in my looks. Finally, he stopped, looked around and said to me, "Well, was I kidding? Have you ever seen anything like this before?"

I didn't answer with words. I just shook my head in the normal "no" answer.

"Richard, these are all things she has started and never finished. Look around; how would you live in this? I can't take it, AND this isn't all of it. We live in a three story house and each floor and the basement is like this."

There was this pause as we just looked at each other. "Don't get me wrong," he said. "Jackie is a great person who lives with good intentions. She really means to finish what she starts when she starts it, but just won't do it. Do you think there is any hope that she can overcome this behavior?"

"It will depend," I said. "It will depend on whether she is willing to face herself and confront the procrastination she has made acceptable for her life. If she is willing to do that, yes there is hope. If she is not willing to face her behavior and work on discipline, there is nothing that can be done."

It took two years, but Jackie is now a recovering procrastinator. If you visited their home today, you wouldn't find any stacks. She has matured to understand the importance of time and how procrastination is a time thief. She understands the things you put off until tomorrow creates the majority of the confusion and frustration you will face. She understands how much energy is drained from you each time you create a stack and have to look at it. Each time you look at it remains an incomplete part of your life.

Isn't it amazing how procrastination can become an acceptable behavior? It is one that many just joke about. The world of good intentions has become an acceptable world.

No one wants to talk about the mental and emotional drain procrastination creates. We sweep it under the carpet with statements like:

- *It's no big deal; I'll get it done.*
- *It's on my list to get to; don't worry.*
- *Hey, I'm sorry; things have just been out of control. It will get done.*
- *I have tomorrow to finish it.*

If you really study these, they give you a good definition of procrastination:

*Procrastination is the behavior of avoidance made acceptable with justifications, reasons, excuses and good intentions.*

The key is understanding it is the behavior of avoidance. You really don't procrastinate because of time; time becomes the excuse. You procrastinate because you don't want to do it. The result is an incomplete event that doesn't go away. It remains an open file in your mind and increases the stress about getting it done.

You really don't procrastinate because there is too much to do. Doing is a choice. You procrastinate because you don't want to do it. Having a lot to do becomes the reason it is okay I didn't get it done. The result is an increase in your anxiety, which feeds your negative stress.

When you are confronted, you use your reasons, excuses and justifications to avoid taking responsibility for your behavior. The result is an increase in your stress and the stress of those who know what you are doing.

When you feel guilty, you apologize for your behavior

and promise to stop procrastinating. That will last until the next thing appears you don't want to do. Then, you revert back to your behavior of avoidance called procrastination.

Procrastination is such a damaging behavior. It keeps all who are caught up in it trapped in an exhausting circle. It is a paralyzing behavior. Until things are completed there can be no forward movement. Just another draining walk through the circle of sameness.

People who procrastinate know this. They just choose to avoid facing it. Have you ever wondered why we procrastinate? In some research I did with a group of compulsive procrastinators here are the common reasons we discovered:

- P  proper planning wasn't done up front
- R  reasons become stronger than desire
- O  others have planned your journey
- C  cluttered with unfinished starts
- R  rationalizing has become okay
- A  a fear of confrontation
- S  sadness
- T  the beginning excitement wears off
- I  involved in the wrong journey
- N  no sense of urgency prevails
- A  a tired spirit
- T  tomorrow becomes the focal point
- E  environment doesn't hold you accountable

If you were to use these as a checklist, how many would be true about you? How many would define your behavior of procrastination?

Can you see how procrastination adds to your negative stress? Can you understand how avoiding things just makes it more challenging to face them?

As long as you make it okay to procrastinate, you will be trapped in repeating the things you have chosen to avoid. Avoidance doesn't make things go away. Avoidance just increases the stress that is hanging around the incomplete event.

To control this stressful behavior you have to face it as your enemy, not your reason. It is important you understand this statement. All improvement begins with "facing what is." Until you can do that, you will always be a hostage to your behavior. You can always see when someone is not facing their life. They will avoid through reasons, excuses, blame and good intentions. These are simply words spoken to deny personal responsibility. This is just a continuation of your procrastination.

This is not about eliminating procrastination from your life. That won't happen. Remember my philosophy? *People who work to eliminate stress become stressful. Those who learn to control their stress enhance their creativity.*

It is not about eliminating procrastination. It is something you will always be challenged by. The key is learning to control its affect on your life.

**How Do You Learn To Control Procrastination?**

C   confront issues, don't avoid them
O   organize yourself to take proper action
N   not making tomorrow your focal point
T   take things at a manageable pace
R   reach for results, not reasons
O   offer no excuses
L   learn the right skills and implement them

## IT'S HERE SOMEWHERE
*Disorganized people are stressful to self and others.*

Well, have you gathered the reality of stress? I am constantly amazed how many don't take it seriously. They joke about the pressure they are under. They know they should do something about the stress that is playing havoc with their life, BUT I guess they don't respect their life enough to take it seriously.

Have you figured out that stress is an emotion triggered by behavior? That means that positive behavior triggers good stress, and bad behavior triggers negative stress.
The positive stress is good for you. When stress is controlled, you find you are at your best. Good stress is where you draw much of your creativity from. I know when I am feeling creative, I can't wait to get to the computer and work. I like that feeling; it pushes me to do more and be better.

Negative stress is not good for you. It wears you down; it attacks you mentally, emotionally and physically. It breaks you down and takes life away from you.

Controlling stress is all about knowing yourself and facing your behavior. It is about being honest with the design of your life. It is about facing those behaviors that steal your energy. One of those behaviors that is so draining is disorganization. *Disorganized people are dysfunctional.* Disorganized people are a drain to others who surround their life. They keep things out of sync; they keep others hanging in limbo unable to move forward with their life.

As she approached me, I could see the tears in her eyes. Wiping her eyes, she said, "All you had to do was say the word *disorganization* and I started crying. You are looking at the

*Disorganized people are dysfunctional people.*

poster child for disorganization. It is not part of my life; it rules my life."

There was a long pause and she calmed herself. "I am so tired of the way my life is. I am so dysfunctional. I don't have the energy to do anything, BUT everywhere I turn there is something for me to do. I don't get anything finished. I start it, touch it, push it aside, touch it again, push it aside and touch it again. Let me tell you how bad it is. I was going through a stack of stuff I felt I had to get finished and found a letter from last year. Now, tell me that's not dysfunctional. This is no way to live, and I know I am not living. I also know I can't go on this way. It is wearing me out. Every stack is just another pile of stress for me. Everything I touch and don't finish is just something else for me to worry about."

"Sarah, have you always been this way?"

"NO! That's the irony to all this. I used to be the most organized person you would ever want to meet. I mean there were no stacks; things were done on time and before they were due. This has just been the last few years. I don't know what happened."

"Did you go through some trauma in your life? I mean did something happen that turned your world upside down?"

"Well, the company I had worked for for twenty-one years let me go. They were going through some financially rough times, and I was one of the highest paid people there. I guess they figured they could replace me for about one-third the money. I was so shocked. I really thought I would retire with them."

There was a long pause, and I knew she was reflecting on what had happened.

"It was a real shock to me. I didn't know what I was

119

going to do. It took me a while to find a job. It's an okay job, but not what I thought I would be doing. I think I have become like so many I see. I just get up, go to work and spend my day doing a job. God, I said I would never be like that. I hate hearing myself say what I have become."

Disorganization is a behavior! It is something you have to choose to be. As I listened to Sarah's story, I learned some things about her.

I learned that her passion for her new job was questionable. This was not what she had seen herself doing with her life. She had this picture of her work life ending with her retiring from the company she had invested years in helping. In a brief moment that all changed.

From her story I also learned her new job required things she did not enjoy doing. There were things about the new job that have become things she "had" to do. She did them because they were part of the job, but that didn't mean she enjoyed doing them.

I also learned that she had become a reactor. The emotional trauma she had gone through had rewritten the script she was using to interrupt her life. Where she once felt secure, now she felt uncertain. Where she once felt safe, now she questioned everything that was happening. Where she felt she was family, was now a divorce she hadn't asked for.

The most telling was the damage that had been done to her spirit. She was wounded and the wounds were deep. Her presence told me she felt betrayed. She had given her spirit to the company and the action that was taken had told her it wasn't appreciated.

Put all this together and you had a picture of a Sarah who was out of sync with herself. Her life had been rearranged without her permission; her dream had been stolen and she wasn't sure what to do.

Know what? Sarah is no different from many who have lost their sense of purpose, been pushed in a direction they didn't want to go, had a chapter handed their life they didn't anticipate being part of their life.

A common aspect of a life that is out of sync is a time of becoming dysfunctional. One of the most common aspects of that dysfunctional time is disorganization.

Let me show you something. It is really easy to paint a picture of a dysfunctional person. Watch!

- *They procrastinate.*
- *They excuse their behavior*
- *They refuse to take responsibility.*
- *They say "I'm sorry," but do the same thing again.*
- *They never finish things in a timely fashion.*

Does any of this sound familiar to you? What do you think this will do to your stress level?

When a person isn't happy with their life, they will be disorganized. Why? Without happiness nothing seems to matter.

When a person has buried their dream, they will be disorganized. Why? Without a dream there is nothing of value to work on.

When a person doesn't have a solid foundation of self worth, they will be disorganized. Why? When you don't like yourself, what difference does it make what you do or don't do.

Disorganization is really a statement about who you see yourself as, where you are in your life and what you feel about what you are doing with your life.

Can you see where disorganization is more than just not

getting things done? It is a personal statement about you and the picture you have of your life.

Do you have any idea how many times I have heard:

- *It doesn't matter what I do; it's not going to make a difference.*
- *Why spend the energy getting this done when I don't enjoy doing it.*
- *I'm so tired of going in circles; I just don't have the energy to face things.*

Disorganization feeds your negative stress. It makes your life one giant trash can that keeps getting filled with what you don't want to do. The more there is in the trash can, the greater the negative stress in your life. Yet, you tell yourself "I'll get it done." What you fail to understand is when you feed disorganization, you create a negative emotional collision that produces long lasting emotional damage. Disorganization creates a heap of negative stress.

**How Do You Get Yourself Organized?**

O   open yourself to the truth about your behavior.

R   respond, don't let yourself react.

G   get yourself moving at the right pace.

A   address issues while they are concerns.

N   no more "to do" list; start achieving.

I   invest in knowledge.

Z   zeal and passion must drive your life.

E   expectations must be in sync with your dream.

D   discipline yourself to do what needs to be done.

# EMOTIONAL STORMS
*If you can't control your personal tiredness, you can't control your stress.*

Have you ever had that sinking feeling? You knew something was wrong, but you felt you couldn't do anything about it. It was like the harder you tried to get beyond it, the deeper you slipped into this giant hole of personal depression. As much as you didn't want to sink, everything you grabbed for wouldn't hold you. Nothing you did would lift you out. All the things you had tried before that had worked now produced a failed attempt. The feeling inside you said, "I can't hang on anymore." Have you ever been there?

If you have you understand what I am talking about. It is one giant feeling of being lost within yourself and not being able to see the road out of the jungle.

It is a feeling of being emotionally overwhelmed. There are so many emotions running wild inside you. You can't stop and just deal with one, because the others just keep dragging you down.

It is like the life is being sucked out of you. All you want to do is sleep, but when you try to sleep, you can't. Your emotions won't turn off. You lie in bed and just toss and turn. If you do fall asleep, you don't sleep long. You awaken feeling exhausted. You want to go back to sleep, but you are awake and restless.

Stress will do this to you! When stress takes over your life and attacks you from the inside out, you are out of control. As hard as you might try to get beyond it, you can just feel yourself sinking deeper and deeper into this dark cavern.

Depression is such a draining event. It sucks life out of

123

If a person could just slow
down and face their life,
they could avoid most of the
emotional storms in their life.

you and leaves these emotional sinkholes all over your life.

Depression is like a dark cloud hanging over your life and everywhere you look there is nothing but dark clouds. You know deep within yourself there is sunshine above the clouds, but you don't have the energy to reach that high. The result is a feeling of hopelessness; a feeling of despair. You can feel the pressure building inside you and there are moments when you think you are going to explode.

Have you ever been here? It is not fun. It is one of life's experiences that causes you to doubt if life has any good moments left for you.

Darcia is thirty, married and the mother of four children. Her life has not been a rose garden. As she put it, "I wanted roses, but got a lot of weeds that grew so fast I couldn't control them."

I met her and Ray at a Quixtar meeting I was doing in South Florida. I finished my program and was at the product table when they approached.

Ray looked at Darcia and she poked him in the ribs as she was saying, "Go ahead ask him. He won't bite you."

I heard what was being said, so I paused, walked over to the end of the table, looked at Ray and said, "Okay! What is it she wants you to ask me?"

He turned red, looked at her and smiled. "We know you are busy and probably don't have time, but if you did, would you spend a few minutes with us. We are really messed up and don't know what to do."

Darcia stepped forward and with a great amount of intensity in her voice said, "We're sinking. We're holding onto our last rope and if it breaks, we are finished."

I knew by the tone of her voice and the intensity of her

words, she was not kidding. "What are you doing at 7:30 this evening?"

They looked at each other and Ray responded. "I don't think we are doing anything."

"Can you find someone to watch the kids for an hour? If you can I will meet you in the coffee shop and we'll talk."

I've got to tell you; that was one draining conversation. Ray had been hurt on the job and not worked for over a year. On top of that he was fighting with his former employer and workman's comp over getting paid. No one wanted to do anything, and Ray felt he was being left out to dry.

Darcia had been forced to become the primary breadwinner. She had enjoyed selling real estate when it was something she did because she wanted to, not because she had to.

They were like so many young couples. They had financially over extended themselves. It was okay because they were both working. Neither thought Ray would be without a job.

They had bought a new house; the one they had wasn't large enough for a family of six. The mortgage was a little more than they needed, but they were both working. They knew they could do it.

Emotionally, they were so different. Ray was the type that ran away when the pressure increased. He had this nice little emotional cave he would run to. Darcia would talk, but when he was hiding in his cave, he didn't pay any attention to her.

Darcia wanted to confront everything, but when she was tired (which she was 99% of the time) she was out of control. That meant she would scream and throw her own version of a temper fit.

Ray didn't know what to do when she did this, so he just retreated deeper into his cave. All that did was make Darcia scream louder and emotionally push him to come out of the cave.

Nothing got resolved; everything became a continuation that emotionally got connected to the next crisis that came along. Their life had no safe haven; just mine fields that they kept stepping into.

Sinking! That wasn't the half of it. Put on top of all this was Darcia's health. Pressure was not something her body handled well. Each time the pressure increased part of her body would shut down.

"We didn't know what to do," Darcia said. "Everywhere we look all we see is another crisis racing toward us. We had one child that was sick and discovered another who had a major health issue. We finally decided Ray would just stay home and take care of the house and the children. He could help me with my Real Estate business."

That sounded good, but in reality it was not a good design for them. They had amassed so much financial debt they could not be a one-income family. They needed Ray to shoulder part of the financial stress.

As good as Ray was about taking care of the house, he didn't do it the way Darcia took care of it. She would walk in after Ray had worked in the house all day and find things she thought he should have taken care of. He didn't do the laundry correctly; he didn't really wash the dishes. On top of all this the girls wanted mom. They were used to having her around. If Darcia tried to work at home, the baby would want her and not Ray.

It was just more pressure than Darcia could handle. Everywhere she turned, everywhere she looked there was simply another crisis racing toward her.

I remember one email she sent me. "Richard, I can't take much more of this. I am being pulled in too many parts. I just want to run away, but I know I can't do that. I feel like I have dropped into that dark abyss we talked about and there is no way out. I can't shoulder all this alone."

I talked to Ray about the pressure she was under and they needed to rethink this design. He needed to step up and take some of the financial pressure off of Darcia.

He didn't get it. His response was, "What is she going to do if I am not here to take care of the house and the kids. Someone has to do it and she doesn't have the time or the energy. I am helping her, but she just can't see it."

Yes, in many ways he was helping her, but he was not taking pressure off her. He was adding to her already overloaded condition.

Finally, late one night Darcia reached her breaking point. She physically attacked Ray, took the baby and left. Ray had no idea where she was or what she was doing. As any person who loves another would be, he was scared, nervous and frightened.

I knew what she was doing. When Darcia was at her end, she would get in the van and just drive. The van represented the only place in her life where she could get away from all the pressure that was consuming her life.

When we finally talked, she was an emotional puzzle with pieces lying all over the place.

"I can't believe I did what I did. I am so ashamed of myself. I don't know if I can ever forgive myself. I have let everyone down."

"Darcia, we talked about the possibility of this happening. You just kept pushing and pushing yourself. Everywhere you look, anyplace you go all you can see is what someone wants or needs from you. It is too much for you to emotionally handle. You have reached the edge and fallen into the sink hole."

"I know, but I should have been stronger. I should have been able to control things."

"You are not super woman. You can't do everything. This was inevitable. The key is to slow down and learn from what happened. Not just you, but Ray. He was a big part of you falling into the sinkhole. He was there, but wasn't there; he was working to help you, but actually emotionally pushed you over the edge. This was not just you; this was a complication of several emotional storms in your life colliding. When they did, the emotional explosion was too great and you snapped."

What do you think would happen to most people who thought they were living on top of the mountain, but the mountain was living on top of them? Do you think most people could handle the pressure? Do you think most people would, in their own way, snap?

I see it everyday. I see people who don't deal with the stress in their life; they simply work to collect more. They don't unload their emotional collection; they add to it. At some point in their life, they snap. The emotions from all they are facing collide and create the perfect emotional storm. Once the emotional storms merge, there is nothing they can do to stop the explosion. They lose it. In their own way they snap and sink into their own form of depression.

Most know it is happening, but for some strange reason think they are strong enough to handle it. What they can't face is all the emotional damage that has been done along the way. They are actually an emotional wreck waiting to collide with their self.

If a person could just slow down and face their life, they could avoid many of these emotional storms. All Darcia and Ray needed to do was slow down and take an honest look at the journey they were planning. If they had, they could have avoided the storms colliding. They, like so many others, don't understand the emotional toll these storms do to your life. They don't just pass through; they sweep through, steal your energy, leave you weak, and then, return with you less able to handle them. At some point your emotional foundation will not be strong enough to handle the sweeping through of the emotional storms and YOU WILL SNAP.

It is important you understand. As strong as you think you may be, run or avoid issues in your life and they will chase you down with a vengeance and emotionally attack you.

The negative stress they attack with will be so great it can mentally, emotionally and physically wipe you out. The key is not to collect emotional issues. The understanding is the necessity to confront issues as they are happening in your life. The strength is the ability to be honest with yourself and not play the games that give the emotional storms time to form. It is important everyone be connected through a common agenda of support.

## How Do You Handle These Emotional Storms?

S    slow down
T    tackle issues as soon as they appear
O    offer no excuses or blame
R    refuse to react to life's situations
M    make all involved take responsibility
S    stay focused on finding resolution

## CRACKED FOUNDATION

*When you don't trust yourself, you will make decisions that will add stress to your life.*

Stress is a fact that forms the sight plan you use to define life's events. When you see the events as positive, you respond with positive energy. When you see the events as negative, you react with negative energy.

Energy carries with it behavior. The behavior you implement designs the journey you will take through, around or avoiding the situation. These are all your choices.

The decision you make is guided by how much you trust yourself. If you trust yourself, you move forward with confidence. You believe you can find the good in this situation and learn from its presence in your life.

If you don't trust yourself, you will worry about what could happen, doubt you can handle it and work to either avoid facing the situation or run as fast as you can for cover.

All of this comes back to your ability to trust yourself. Trust is one of the most important principles of personal growth that there is. The opposite of trust is fear. It is important you understand this. If you don't trust yourself, you will design your life to be guided by fear. When this happens, you live in a world where negative stress will have control of your life.

Anytime I work with a person, one of the first assessments I have to make is *how much do they trust self.* I know my ability to guide them toward growth is dependent on personal trust.

Trust is one of the foundations to personal growth. Without trust doubt has an open door to your life. Without trust you will second-guess your life and constantly be increasing

133

The opposite of trust is fear.
One of the two is always in
control of the design of your life.

the pressure you are wrestling with.

Without trust the unknown will become one of those hurdles you will be tripping over. Trust is needed to step through the doorway of sameness into a world that is not always predictable. The unknown is always an event filled with negative fear when self-trust is not part of your solid foundation.

Without a solid foundation of self-trust you will wrestle with self worth. I have said for years I think self worth is more important than self-confidence or self esteem. Both self-confidence and self-esteem are by-products of self worth.

When Justin approached me, he had this big smile on his face and was shaking his head from side to side. "I don't know if I should like you or hate you" were his opening words to me. "You said you would get inside us and play and boy did you do it to me. I am exactly the person you were talking about tonight. I have struggled most of my life with trusting myself."

There was a long pause and the smile that appeared on his face now turned to a look of disappointment. "Richard, I am talented, I am creative, but I am my own worst enemy. I know what I want to do, but every time I get excited this little voice inside me takes over, and I stop short of reaching my goal. I know it is all about not trusting myself."

"Justin, most of our lack of self trust can be tied to a fear that has control of our life. Remember me talking about the six negative fears tonight?"

"Yes! That really grabbed me and made me stop and look at myself."

"Which one of the six, fear of the unknown, abandonment, failure, rejection, loss or success do you think you wrestle with the most?"

"Oh, that's the easy part. It's the fear of failure. My dad was a perfectionist and thought his kids should also be a perfectionist. None of us could ever please him. Since I was the only boy, I got the worst of it. No matter how good my grades were, they were never good enough. I remember when I was in the eighth grade. I spent time working on my science project. I was really proud of it. My dad came into my room the night before the project was due, looked at it and told me it was a piece of junk. Richard, that is like a burning ember in my mind. It was like that event sucked all my self-belief out. I went from a person who had confidence to a person who didn't trust anything they tried to do. I started doubting every thought I had; I would always second-guess myself and in doing so would walk away before I completed things. I have become a person who lives by blame, excuses, reasons, and justification — all those things you were talking about tonight. I am tired of living this way; I don't want this type of life anymore."

If Justin's dad only knew what he had done to his son. The second most important foundation in life is self-trust. With it you take risk; with it you have confidence; with it, you are willing to reach for the horizon, BUT when it is cracked, it opens you to all the negative doubts and worries life can throw at you.

Self-trust forms the foundation for your dreams. When you trust yourself you believe in the ideas your imagination creates for you.

I wish you could meet Lisa. She is one neat lady. She will tell you "I haven't always been this way. For years I lost my ability to trust myself. I slipped into a behavioral style where I lived controlled by worry and doubt. I got up each day waiting for the next crisis to attack my life. I didn't know me

136

and furthermore I didn't like who I had become."

Lisa was raised by parents who didn't believe in limitations. They had instilled in all their children to trust self and reach for their dreams. When Lisa was in high school, she was Miss Everything. Everybody saw Lisa as a girl who "had it all." In fact in her High School Yearbook those were the words most often used to describe her.

In college Lisa excelled. She was in the top 2% of her class. She was bright; she was creative; she was driven; there was nothing she couldn't do. She had her life planned. She was going to be the best product marketing person the business world had ever seen. She caught the eye of a major PR Agency and was hired before she even graduated from college. They were so impressed with her spirit and drive they had already started creating plans for her.

Then Lisa met Randy. Randy was everything that Lisa wasn't. He came from a very dysfunctional family where he was kicked out of the house when he was seventeen. His parents told him to never come back, and he hadn't seen them since. He dropped out of school his senior year and took a job working for a produce company. He wasn't happy there, but it provided him with money. There was nothing in his life he was happy about.

He really was the opposite of Lisa. If you were to put him in a group and pick the least likely person for Lisa, it would have been Randy.

One of Lisa's college friends was a friend of one of the guys Randy hung with. One night at a party they met and Lisa was emotionally taken by Randy. They started dating and after a year got married. Those who were close to Lisa, including her parents, tried to talk to her, but there was no talking to Lisa about Randy.

The marriage lasted for two years. As I worked with Lisa, it became apparent to her she didn't marry Randy because she loved him; she married him to rescue him from the terrible life he had had. The reality was in trying to rescue him, she started to drown.

Randy hated Lisa's positive spirit and would take every opportunity to bring her down. He hated the fact she had a job she loved and caused so much havoc for her that she lost her job. He didn't like her positiveness and made such a fuss Lisa stopped seeing her parents. He really didn't like her parents. Anytime they were around, it became an emotional war. He told her she would have to choose between seeing them and being with him. Slowly, Lisa started pulling away from them.

One day Lisa woke up, looked in the mirror and saw this old woman looking back at her. Here was a young lady, whose eyes used to be filled with sparkle, now looking lifeless. Here was this young lady whose imagination used to work overtime creating ideas, now not having the energy to even think. Here was this beautiful young lady who once enjoyed living, now involved in a relationship that had sucked the life out of her.

"Richard," she said during our first visit. "I don't like who I have become. I want the me I used to be back. I am not sure I can ever get back to being that person who trusted herself, was willing to take risk and was in love with life. I am so far removed from that person; I am not even sure she is still alive."

Over a period of a year we gave Lisa her life back. It wasn't easy. The negative Lisa had established such a foothold in her life that we had to fight long and hard to put her away.

It wasn't easy because we had to edit a lot of tapes Randy had programmed her with.

Thank goodness her parents had not given up on her. They had her move back into their house and helped to rebuild her spirit of self-trust. They became her cheerleaders. It wasn't always easy. They had to put up with the times she would slip back into the negative Lisa, but their love for her kept them solid in their commitment to helping her rediscover who she was.

Today Lisa is back being her creative self. She is working for a PR firm and has been given several of their top clients. She is alive and filled with the spirit of self-trust. She is alive and stands on a firm foundation of self worth.

She told me recently, "I didn't think I could get back here. I was so lost; I was so down on myself; I was living a life where I had died, but hadn't laid down in the casket yet. I can't believe I did that to myself. What was wrong with me?"

There are a lot of Lisa's out there. There are also a lot of Randy's out there. No matter how strong your self-worth is *if you hang around with the Randy's of life long enough, they will suck the life out of you.*

Self-trust offers you calmness. When you are calm, you can handle the stressors of life. Take the calmness away and the stressors handle you.

Self-trust connects to self worth. When you see yourself as a person of value, you live as a person of value. When you lack self worth, you lack personal value. All your behaviors are designed to say, "I am not valuable."

Self-trust gives you a solid foundation to stand on during life's challenges. You will be challenged, and each challenge is a test of how much you believe in you. With self-trust you pass the test and arrive with a stronger picture of personal value and worth. This is where you are at your best.

Self-trust is about self respect! Watch any person and see how they treat their self. Study the words they use to define their life; watch how they handle the little surprises that come to their life and you have a picture of who they see their self as, what they feel about their life and what their future will offer them. .

When you trust yourself, you respect your mind. You see it as your friend and the power to excel at your dream.

When you trust yourself, you guide your emotions, rather than them guiding you. That grants you control of your life's direction.

When you trust yourself, you surround your life with others who share the self-trust. This allows you to sharpen your skills and fine tune your thinking. It grants you the joy of being with people who bring strength to your life.

Without self-trust you will stand on a foundation where the cracks are always redefining life through its wrongs. Without self-trust you will wake up each day struggling with what life "isn't." You will become a stressed mess.

## How Do You Develop This Self-Trust?

T    truth about self and what is in your life
R    reach out to those who offer strength
U    unmask the fears that hold you hostage
S    see the value your life brings
T    there must be emotional calmness

## How Did I Get Here?
*Staying in the wrong place makes life very stressful.*

No matter where you turn, there is going to be stress. No matter what part of life you are talking about, there is going to be stress. Stress is one of the most consistent factors of life. That said, you cannot forget that *as natural as stress is, it is also as dangerous.* This book is focusing on learning to control the negative aspects of stress.

Stress is an emotion that appears as a result of the collision of events in your life. Every event carries some element of stress. The level is defined by how you handle the situation you are dealing with. If you face it head on, you can control the level of stress. That doesn't mean there aren't going to be emotional moments where you will wrestle with what is about to happen. It means as you face it, you move through and don't give the negative aspects of stress time to establish a damaging presence in your life.

When you choose (and it is a choice) to avoid the situation, you open yourself to the gathering of negative emotions which will increase your negative stress, which will fill your life with negative emotional drain. That is when stress becomes unhealthy and dangerous.

I can't say this enough to you. *Stress doesn't have to be a damaging part of your life.* It is very important you understand this. Stress is a fact that is ever present. The mission is not you working to eliminate the stress, BUT learning to *control* the stress in your life.

The longer you allow events to gather emotions the more challenging it becomes to control the stress. Most of the damage is the result of you either avoiding the situation or

*Nothing in your life can improve until you take responsibility for what you have done.*

denying its existence in your life. These two cause many to ask the question, *"How did I get here?"*

Have you ever been here? I mean you were so stressed out you didn't know what was going on. One day your life was doing okay. THEN, out of nowhere came this storm filled with negative stress. You really didn't see it coming, but you felt its arrival. It blew through your life and turned a good day into a stressful day.

It just seemed to come out of nowhere and turned a seemingly calm situation into one that was out of control. The result was you and everyone else involved stressed out.

You found yourself worn out, beat down, frustrated, controlled by worry and trying to figure out "what happened." What was left of you just wanted to run away and hide before the storm came back. Does this sound familiar to you?

It was around 6:30 in the morning and I was sitting in the lobby of the Marriott in Maui. I had my coffee, my computer, the beach and a beautiful sunrise. What more could a man want out of life?

I was staring off into the distance when I was brought back by this voice talking to me. "Well, I see you are an early riser also."

I turned to see this gentleman standing beside me looking off into the distance. "Yes, I am. Why sleep when you can be awake and enjoying life."

"Richard, I hope I am not bothering you. I sort of figured you would be around here somewhere working on your computer. Would you mind if I joined you for a moment? I promise not to take a lot of your time, but I have a question I would like to ask you."

I pointed to the chair and he sat down. "So," I said,

"What is going on inside your head?"

" A lot," he said in a much different voice than he had been speaking in. "My life is really messed up."

He repositioned himself in his chair, and I knew he was simply gathering his thoughts before he continued.

He looked at me with pain in his eyes and continued. "I really had a difficult time with you yesterday. You were preaching to me. I was the person you were talking about whose life was running him, rather than me managing my life. I wanted to get up and leave, but I knew I needed to hear what you were talking about. I'll tell you something. It isn't easy to sit there and have someone, who doesn't know you, read your life and emotionally turn you upside down."

There was this long pause. I figured he was trying to muster up the courage to ask the question that had caused him to seek me out.

"Richard, do you think it is possible to put your life back together after you have royally screwed it up?"

I turned so he had to look at me and said, "It is always possible to put your life back together. That is not the challenge. The challenge is being honest enough to face what you have done and learn enough not to repeat it."

"But..."

I cut him off before he could complete his thought. "Don't like the word but. It is a conjunction that is generally followed by an excuse, a reason or a justification. None of those will help you. They are only designed to keep you moving in the same exhausting circle of drain."

"You're right. I do that all the time. I can't believe I have messed my life up so much. I don't know how I got here. No, that's not true. I know how I got here. I just don't want to admit I was the one who was the problem."

"Hey," I said. "You're on the right track. At least you are now willing to take responsibility for where you are. That's where it has to start. Nothing in your life can improve until you take responsibility for what you have done."

The stress in your life is the result of decisions you have made, not the situation you were handed. The situation provided you with the opportunity to choose a path. Filtering into your decisions were emotions. Those emotions created your feelings and in turn formed your beliefs about what was happening.

If you really slowed down and learned with every decision there is a journey, you would spend more time investigating, rather than having to emotionally clean up what your behavior has created. It goes back to you managing your life, rather than your life managing you.

It's the difference between you responding, rather than reacting. So much of life's confusion, which results in stress, is the result of you moving at a pace you can't manage. If you can't manage your life, it will manage you. That is a fact!

When life is managing you, you will react. Each event your life is handed will be viewed through emotional filters, not through your mind seeking understanding. Without understanding you will emotionally speed up and only want to get through the event.

The quick fix mentality is one of the best ways to increase the stress in your life. 99% of the things you "fix" you will have to come back and emotionally wrestle with again. That is pure exhaustion. The more exhausted you become the greater your personal stress. Why? When you are exhausted, you can't make a decision. You can only touch the moment.

The result is an emotional circle that keeps requiring more and more of your energy.

     The key is pace. The faster you move the more challenging your life becomes. You can't race through a situation without doing emotional damage. The emotional damage will generate stress. The stress will take and not give back. That just opens you up to more turmoil in your life. At some point you will pause and ask yourself *how did I get here?* The answer is really locked into your behavior, not the event you were challenged with. Slow down and respond and issues can be resolved and moved beyond. Speed up and react and the issue grows in its emotional presence. That means it controls you, rather than you controlling the issue. The result is negative stress increasing its presence, and you becoming emotionally weaker. At that point your life becomes a feasting ground for negative stress.

**How Do You Learn To Slow Down?**

    S    stop and take that deep breath
    L    look at your fears
    O    open yourself to getting help
    W   walk, don't run

# THIS IS A TEST

*Every situation in life provides you with a test. Your behavior determines whether you get through or have to repeat the event.*

Who is your #1 enemy? In reality do you wrestle more with the situations your life is handed, or with yourself?

The situations your life is handed are not the enemy; they are the test. The test will provide the opportunity to either grow or cause you to fall backward and have to repeat the event.

I am constantly asked, "Why can't I get beyond this?" The answer is really simple. *You are free from the struggles in life when you pass the test and have learned how to deal with them.*

That is so challenging for most people to understand. They don't understand the concept of the "test." They really don't understand the concept of "living a journey." If they understood the concept of test and journey, they would look at life through a different set of emotional filters. They would not make their life a race; they would not look around to see who they could blame; they would not seek the shortest route.

If they understood the idea of test and journey, they would seek to find the lesson that is part of every situation their life is handed. They would find, learn and implement those lessons into their life. It is through the finding, learning and implementing you control the level of stress your life faces on a daily basis.

One of the greatest aspects of drain on the human life is having to repeat an event that has already stolen energy from you. The repeating of any stressful event increases the

Life is not about what you are handed; life is about what you do with what you are facing.

level of stress and adds to your personal frustration. As the frustration grows, it turns into personal disappointment. As the disappointment takes hold, it makes you question yourself. When you start questioning yourself, you open your life to increased worry, increased doubt and second guessing yourself. You talk about a life that is out of control!

This can be taken away by understanding the concept of test and journey. When you can see life's situations as a test for you to slow down and walk through, you learn lessons that grant you control. When you understand your behavior in any situation creates the journey the situation brings to your life, you see the importance of responding with calmness and clarity, rather than reacting with speeding up and seeking to avoid. The difference between the two creates the mental sight you are able to bring to the event. Reality is, the faster you move the less mental sight you have and the stronger your emotional presence becomes. The slower you move the more mental strength you have and the less emotional control the situation has over your life.

As much as she doesn't like to admit it, Janie is an emotional reactor. Here is a life that is in a constant state of crisis. In the time I have known her I have not seen one day that was not guided by her emotions running wild. The simplest thing becomes a major point of conflict and confusion.

I met her and her husband, Jeff, at a convention I was speaking at in St. Louis. They had come by while I was gone and asked my staff if they could have some time with me. When I returned, Clarita pointed them out to me. I walked over to where they were seated, sat down, looked at them and began. "So, you need some time with me. Well, I am yours for the next few minutes. What is happening with the two of you?"

They looked at each other with this stunned look on

their face and then, Janie spoke up. "Everything is happening with us. We are so out of control with our life and with each other that we have no life. Everywhere I turn there is another crisis for me to take care of."
Jeff interrupted Janie with, "Well, it's not really that bad."

With fire in her eyes Janie jumped back into the conversation. "Oh yea! Then, tell me one part of our life that is not in crisis. Go ahead, tell me?"

The look on Jeff's face told me he wasn't sure how to respond to her. You could tell she was the emotional leader in this relationship. His head dropped, and I could see through his body language he was finished with this conversation.

There was this long silence as Janie stared at him. When she saw he had withdrawn, she looked at me and continued. "My life has not always been this way. Years ago I lived in a very calm environment and didn't have all this crap to deal with on a daily basis. Then, I gave into his pressure to get married. I didn't want to, but he was relentless and I finally caved in. Since that day twelve years ago, I haven't had a life. I have existed in this upside down hell that has taken my life away from me."

"Janie," I said as I leaned in toward her. "First of all, no one can take your life away from you. You have to surrender it. Second, no one can force you to do anything. All behavior is a choice. Third, your life is not guided by others; it's guided by what you choose to do. It seems you are making Jeff responsible for what you don't want to take responsibility for."

I wish you could have seen Jeff perk up. It was like someone for the first time had taken his side. His head popped up, he sat up straight in the chair and it was as if a light came on in his eyes.

"Janie," I continued. "Life is the result of what we choose to do with the situations we are handed. Every situation is a test of our growth and our commitment to either improving or continuing the pain in our life. What you do with the test determines the journey you get to travel. Most people don't want to take personal responsibility, so they look around and see who and what they can blame. As long as there is something or someone to blame, they feel they have an escape. Reality is, they don't have an escape; they simply have a guarantee of the continuation of the stress in their life."

I promise you that was not what she wanted to hear. There was fire in her eyes, and I could tell I had really made her mad. The look on her face told me she didn't know what to say. The silence was deafening and the tension was intense.

"You didn't want to hear that, did you?"

There was not an answer; just a continuation of her stare. I waited to see if the stare would soften, but it didn't."

"Janie, you are a very emotionally charged young lady. Your presence tells me you have given your emotions control of your life. That is a big part of the challenge you are facing. As long as your emotions are guiding you, your mind takes a back seat. When your mind is in the back seat, you don't have direction. All you have is this exhausted circle you travel. That means you don't get through anything. Everything just keeps repeating itself in your life. Is that a pretty good picture of your life?"

She didn't get to answer before Jeff jumped in with "That's her alright. She is never calm. She is always fighting some battle. If there is no battle, she will find one. She keeps me and the kids in a defensive mode. That is so exhausting and keeps the kids guessing what is going to happen next."

151

Janie glared at him. "I guess others must think that's the way I am. I just see myself as a tired person who is worn out from fighting the fires in my life that never end. I wish I could just have one day that didn't stress me out."

"Janie, that's the test! You can have that day. It is there for you each and every day of your life. You have to create it and then live it. Reality is, you must not want it enough to fight for it. You get up and give into whatever your day throws at you. The events of the day are there to test what you really want for your life. If you want a calm life, you can have it. If you want a life that is upside down and constantly draining you of energy, you can have that to. Either is there for you; you must see the test and choose the answer."

"You make it sound so simple."

"Janie, it is. You are the one who makes it difficult. You choose what you want for your life and then, live it out through your behavior. It is not Jeff; it is not the kids; it is not your job; it is not what your life is handed. It is YOU! You make the choice; you decide what you will see; you choose whether you will react emotionally or respond mentally. You have just gotten into the behavior of reacting emotionally and then, looking for someone or something to blame. That has become your living design and with that living design comes the journey you are living. If you are tired of that, you can get out. It won't be easy, but you can break out of this emotional prison you have created for yourself."

That conversation started a year journey with Janie and Jeff. Today their life is better; today Janie has slowed down and is learning the difference between reacting and responding to life. Today, she understands the idea of test and journey. She doesn't view life's challenges as a problem. She sees them as a test of her commitment to live her life without overwhelming stress. Each time I talk to her I can feel the calmness taking over. Each time I am with the two of them I can see how the emotional war they have been fighting has taken a back seat to the growth they are experiencing together.

Do you know how many Janie's there are out there? They live their life on a collision course with self. They don't have a chance to have a calm presence; they are too busy creating chaos and conflict for their life.

Do you understand how many Jeff's there are out there? They live with an emotional reactor and have surrendered to the emotional pressure that is daily dumped on them. They have no life; they have become a whipping post and each day awaken to the accepted emotional beating.

Do you understand how many Janie's and Jeff's there are out there? They live in a relationship driven by pain, conflict and the blaming of each other for what their life isn't. There mission is to punish each other and they know exactly what to do to achieve that.

Life is not about what you are handed. Life is about what you do with what you are facing. Every event is a test for you to take. That test is about your commitment; it is about your desire; it is about your self-trust; it is about what you really want for your life. If you face and pass the test, you get to move forward. If you face and fail the test, you have to go back and repeat the event. It may not be the same, but the requirements are the same test.

Life really is a series of tests. Each time you take the test, you design the living journey for you. Look at what the journey is offering your life, and you will know if you have passed or failed.

## How Do You Know When You Have Passed The Test?

T    there is a sense of inner peace
E    emotions take a back seat
S    stress decreases
T    there is growth in your life

## No Map

*The lack of a personal dream increases the negative stress in your life.*

Stress really is an emotion that feeds off of other emotions. If the table is set with positive emotions, the result is stress you can manage. If the table is set with negative emotions, the result is negative stress that eats at you from the inside.

One aspect of negative stress that is so important for you to understand is the fact that *confusion is one of the top things negative stress feeds off of.* Confusion is emotional blindness that creates a wall your mind can't see over or through. It leaves you with the feeling of uncertainty. This feeling of uncertainty leaves you questioning what to do. The result is a life paralyzed and stuck in repeating, not moving forward.

Confusion attacks your mind's search for clarity. Your mind is at its best when it can clearly see what is and can map out the plan for getting there. As long as your mind is clear, you can manage the stress that is a natural part of every journey. When confusion takes over as the predominant player, your mind shuts down and you are left to guess at what is happening in your life. That uncertainty will open the door to the arrival and increase in negative stress.

Confusion erodes your confidence and creates the feeling of uncertainty. Uncertainty plays havoc with your self-trust. The weaker your inner feelings of trust the more challenging it becomes to make decisions you believe in. When your life becomes a guessing game, negative stress increases.

Isn't it amazing the vicious circle of drain the negative

Every time you get
out of sync, lose your focus and
feel you are lost, everything that
happens to your life just sucks
energy out of you.

aspects of life creates? Every time you get out of sync, lose your focus and feel you are lost, everything that happens to your life just sucks energy out of you.

Negative emotions use the drain to keep you tired. When you are tired, you tend to accept, rather than question.

When you are tired, you tend to give yourself permission to procrastinate. You can justify the procrastination because you don't have the energy to deal with the situation right now.

When you are tired, you tend to excuse more things in your life. That's okay, because as soon as you get rested, you will take care of it.

Isn't it amazing how much energy the negative takes from you life? The result is you trapped; the result is you uncertain which direction to turn; the result is you standing in your life without a directional map. The result is you being controlled, rather than you being in control.

Larry was one of the most intelligent people I had ever met. He had a very gifted mind, but lacked the self-trust to really challenge his life.

Larry was married to a very successful woman who saw Larry's lack of self-trust as him being lazy. She came from a family where you didn't question yourself; you just believed you could and you did it. Larry worked for her company, but because Laura didn't respect him, neither did the people who worked for her. They followed her lead of feeling sorry for him and never saw the Larry that lived within.

Larry's brother had been in a conference where I had spoken and called me about Larry. He wanted to know if I would call Larry and see if he would be willing to work with me. He had already told Larry about me and wasn't sure how

Larry would receive my call.

It was a Monday afternoon when Denise told me I had a call from a gentleman named Larry. When I answered my phone, the voice on the other end was filled with the sound of uncertainty.

"Mr. Flint, my name is Larry and my brother told me I needed to give you a call. He said if anyone could help me, it would be you."

There was this pause, and I could feel the pain, frustration and sense of loss coming through the telephone line.

"My life is out of control. I exist in a world that is tearing me apart. I don't know who I am, where I am or what I am doing with this thing called life. I am lost and don't have any idea how to get out of this."

"Larry, your brother told me you might be calling. Life is always challenging, but there are times when the challenges we face seem overwhelming."

"Overwhelming is not the word I would use to describe my life. I am in the muck and each day seem to be sinking deeper and deeper. I don't know how much longer I can exist like this. My brother seems to have a lot of faith in you. He said he has heard you several times. He said he called you a year ago when his life was out of control and you were able to help him turn it around. Do you think you can do that with me?"

"I never make promises Larry. It really doesn't depend on me. It depends on how much you want to get out of this muck you say you are living in."

"I want out! That is as strong as I can say it. I want out of this hellhole I have made for myself. My life is nothing but one stressful day after another. I can't. No, I won't go on like this. Will you help me?"

That conversation began a year long journey that was filled with many gut-wrenching conversations. The reality was Larry had always lived a life planned and programmed by others. When he was a boy, his parents planned his life. He didn't get to make any decisions. They were all made for him. It wasn't his dream; it was theirs. It wasn't what he wanted to do; it was what they planned for him. It wasn't what he wanted to do with his life; it was what he was told he would do.

Then, when Larry married Laura, it wasn't what he wanted for a wedding; it was what Laura and her parents wanted. It wasn't what Larry wanted to do with his life; it was what Laura planned for Larry to do. It wasn't whether Larry wanted children; it was that Laura was to have two children.

Larry's entire life was a planned collision. He didn't know how to plan his life; he only knew how to fulfill the wants that others had for him. In the beginning that was okay.

During one of our sessions he said, "For a long time I didn't mind it. I never had to make any decisions. I just showed up and did what others told me to do. During that time in my life there wasn't any real stress, or at least I didn't think there was. I now think I was just fooling myself. I had a lot of pressure. If I didn't live up to what the others planned for me, I got punished. My parents would punish me by not giving me attention. They would give me their look of disappointment and just walk away. Laura would punish me by being my critic. She would remind me of all she and her parents were doing for me."

"Larry, when did all this change?"

"That's a good question. I have tried to put my finger on it, but I can't pinpoint the turning point. I think it started when Laura demoted me from Vice President to just another programmer in the company. She announced it to the entire company at a meeting and told them that I was no long a company Vice President. Her reason was I just wasn't skilled to be Vice President. Richard, I mean she told that to the entire company! I don't ever remember feeling the rage I felt at that moment. That night at home we had the biggest fight we had ever had. It was beyond ugly; it was one where I said things I had kept inside for years. She told me if I didn't like what she did, get a job somewhere else."

"Do you think she was trying to hurt you?"

"I've thought about that. I don't want to think so, but why would she announce it to the entire company? Why didn't she have that conversation with me in private? I would never do that to her."

There was a long moment of silence as he wrestled with the emotions that were racing through him.

"Larry, what are you going to do?"

"I don't know. I have had a company contact me about writing a book. Richard, I am really good at understanding computers. I have spoken at several conferences and been invited back each time. They tell me I have a way of making it so simple that anyone can understand it."

"Do you think you could write a book? Are you disciplined enough to do it?"

"I've never done anything like that. I had never really thought about it, but I like the idea. I just don't know how to start or what I would say."

"Larry, why don't you talk to the company that has asked you about writing the book and see what they have in mind. I think that would be a good starting point. Call them, set up an appointment and see what their expectations are."

That was the start of the journey that belonged to Larry. He not only wrote a book that was a huge success, but has written two others that have made him a household name in certain computer circles. When you talk to Larry today, you see a different person. No longer does he live the plan others have given him. Today, he has his own master plan and is free to really discover what he can achieve with his life.

Reality is *Larry is not the exception; he is the rule.* Society is filled with the Larry's who get up each day and crawl into a world that is not their canvas to paint. They show up each day in arenas that have been pre-planned for them and they fulfill what others have decided their life will be.

Granted, for some that life is okay for them. They don't want to have to think for themselves; they don't want to have to make decisions about life. They just want to show up and move through their circle of sameness. They don't want anyone to mess up their little routine world.

BUT, for others it is not okay. They don't want to be told how they have to live and what they have to do. YET, they are trapped because that is all they have known. They don't enjoy it, but what are they to do? They want out, but the fear of the unknown has them trapped. They sit around with their dreams that have become mere fantasies their mind plays with and their emotions use against them. They really are the world of the trapped. They have been trapped so long many don't believe there is anything else for them. Reality is *without a map they are lost in the muck of their own life.*

What they fail to see is there is always a map. There are always possibilities; there is always an exit. It is just the fact the longer you have been in the muck, the easier it is to accept the muck as all your life will ever be.

What do you think happens to a life that gives up? Do you think there is negative stress here? What do you think happens to a life that loses the faith there is always something better? Do you think there is any negative stress here?

Life was not made for routine existence; life was designed for challenge, for growth, for taking risk, for finding and trusting in your talents. When that is not your life, there is negative stress to hold you hostage.

There is no life without a life map. There is no growth without a plan that pushes you beyond what was acceptable for yesterday. There is no joy without victory. It is all about designing your life for growth, and then growing your life beyond where each day ends.

Now, I am not saying growth doesn't produce stress. Growth does produce stress, but it is stress you can manage. Growth and improvement allows you to see the continued pathway that is in front of you. Yes, there is stress to that, but that stress creates enthusiasm, and that's good!

## How Do You Find Your Road Map?

R    recognize your talents
O    open yourself to risk taking
A    ask the right questions to the right people
D    don't discount yourself
M    move forward, not in circles
A    admit and face your fears
P    plan before you leap

## SURPRISE!
*When life hands you the unexpected, it will increase your personal stress.*

How many times have you heard the statement *when life hands you lemons, make lemonade?* For most that is easier said than done. For most when life hands them lemons, they squeeze the lemons and find the sour part of it. Why? The answer is the emotional sight you approach an event with.

If you are prepared for the event, it is much easier to make lemonade. If the event is a surprise, many react to the lemon and find the sour taste of the lemon. Reality is, most don't handle surprises very well.

Randall put it this way, "I don't like lemons I didn't pick. I am one of those people who likes for their life to be predictable. I want to live in my routine and not have anything disturb the routine I have established for my life. When the routine is disturbed, I am not a happy camper."

How many Randall's do you think there are out there? They want the routine; they want their life to flow with sameness. They feel life is at its best when there is a consistent routine that allows them to predict what is going to happen and when it will take place. When life hands them a lemon, they are out of sync. Out of sync they are not sure what to do or how to handle the interruption to their established routine.

For years people have been taught they need to establish comfortable routines for their life. It is my personal belief that comfortable routines can be both negative and stressful. When you are locked into a comfortable routine, you don't pay attention to what is happening in and around your life. That means you have opened your life to the surprises that

When your emotions are all
over the place, any surprise will
increase your personal stress.

tend to rock a life based on routine. When that life is rocked, it sends the life into emotional shock, which will increase the stress.

A comfortable routine also weakens your ability to respond with thought when the surprise does happen. The stronger the comfortable routine the more reactive your life becomes. Locked into a comfortable routine you tend to move based on what has been; as long as life is repetitive, the less thinking you have to do. Let the comfortable routine be rocked with the unexpected and watch your life gain tension and view the situation through emotions guided by increased stress.

Eric put it this way. "I don't handle surprises very well. My entire life has been based on my ability to create routine. I am at my best when there are no surprises. When I am handed a turn I wasn't expecting, I find myself speeding up and just wanting it to go away. Over the years I have finally realized how many possibilities I have missed. When you are only seeking sameness, you miss the possibilities that are handed your life, which could create a better life. I wish I had understood that years ago. If I had, I would not be in the same place, facing the same challenges and feeling trapped. Rather than my routines helping my life, they have actually made it impossible for me to become what I have always said I wanted to be. I just wish I had learned this earlier."

Eric is like so many who at some point in their life wake up and realize that routine is about protecting what is, rather than being willing to explore what can be. Routine doesn't allow your imagination to challenge you with newness, because routine is about staying the same.

The Circle of Sameness is such a trap. It shuts down your creative spirit and locks you into believing today is as good as it is going to get. Then, when life hands you a left turn, rather than slowing down and examining it, you speed up and race by what you call a surprise. Without realizing it that steals your creative spirit. The human spirit needs newness to grow. The human spirit needs new events to test its strength.

What many don't understand is the difference between a "new event" and a "surprise." A "surprise" is a situation you find yourself dealing with that you are not emotionally prepared for. It hands your life an emotional surge, which tends to speed you up. As you speed up, your emotions gain strength and your mind doesn't get to examine. That means you miss what this situation offers you in the way of opportunity.

Some don't like surprises because their life is already out of control. They are already involved in a race and don't need anything else thrown at them. With their emotions racing when something new is handed their life, it just adds more pressure to the stress they are already experiencing.

A "new event" is a situation handed your life that you see as a step toward gaining insights and information, which will improve your life. You may not always enjoy their arrival, but you see the need for this event. You understand to keep your life moving forward you need to face this event with an open mind and controlled emotions.

Now for the interesting question. *Which of these two do you experience more of in your life?* When life hands you a situation, do you see it as a surprise or a learning experience? Your answer will show you the real emotional design you have for your life.

Life really is not about sameness; it is about seeking new experiences and allowing them to challenge your thinking and push you toward continual improvement. Reality is —

there is less stress in accepting than there is in fighting the events of life.

## How Do You Handle Surprises?

S   slow down

U   unmask your fear about the event

R   refuse to run through it

P   pause and look for the lesson

R   reach out if you can't handle it alone

I   invest in gathering information

S   state your feeling out loud or in writing

E   exit if the pressure gets too great

S   stay at a manageable pace throughout

# Do or Die!
*No joke! Stress can kill you!*

Talk to any medical professional and ask them what damage stress is capable of doing to your life? Ask them about the power of uncontrolled stress? If you do, you had better be prepared to hear their answer. They will tell you in no uncertain terms that *stress can kill you.*

If that is not a wake up call, I don't know what is. If that doesn't grab your attention and make you pay attention to your life's design, then you don't enjoy living. Stress is not something to play with. Stress is not something to joke about. Stress is not something you can take care of tomorrow.

Stress you don't manage, will manage you. It is a friend when you respect it and keep it under control. It is your enemy when you just let it have its way in your life. Negative stress doesn't respect life; negative stress doesn't care about you as a person; negative stress takes and doesn't give back. In fact — *it can take your life!*

So many health issues are created by stress. I was sitting at dinner with Alice and Pete when I noticed this red rash on Alice's neck. She saw me looking at it, turned bright red and said, "Stress! My body is fighting with me. I have had this ever sense this issue started with Marilyn."

Marilyn is their daughter who has become their problem child. She is living with a young man that Alice and Pete don't like. They feel his agenda is to make sure Marilyn has no relationship with them. Since Alice is a fixer, this is more than she can handle. On top of that there are challenges at the firm where Pete works. Alice sees how stressed he is and her worries about both situations have begun to take over her body.

Negative stress doesn't respect your life or care about you as a person. In fact, as an enemy, it will kill you!

*Stress can take a physical toll on your body!*

Ruth came to me with her life upside down. She was married to a controller. He had to have total control of her life. She couldn't make a move without his permission. She finally reached a place where she was no longer willing to live like that. She came to me after a long visit with her doctor.

She looked at me with tears coming down her face and said, "My doctor told me this is killing me. He said if I don't do something about this stress in my life, it is going to kill me. Richard, I can't live this way. My blood pressure is off the charts, I don't sleep, and I cry at the drop of a pin. I have to do something about this."

*Stress can make your body react in some very dangerous ways.*

Shawn had always wanted to own his own business. He was a very creative young man who had a ton of ideas. Each idea he thought was a financial gold mine just waiting for him to put them together. His challenge was his lack of business experience. He didn't understand capital; he didn't understand how to build a business; he just knew he had a great idea. He teamed up with three other gentlemen who thought his ideas were great. None of them had the money, so Shawn ended up using his savings and his credit cards to finance his dream. Three years into the project there was no more savings, no more credit card money and a wife who was totally reactive to what he had done to their family. When he approached the other gentlemen, they couldn't help. In fact they bailed, leaving Shawn to face the financial mess on his own.

He came to me on the recommendation of one of his friends. The minute he entered my life I could sense the stress that had overwhelmed his life. The stress he felt from a sense of failure had pushed his life into depression.

As he sat there staring out the window, he started talking in a very defeated tone. "I can't believe I have done this. I just can't believe I have punished my family with my fantasy. I have taken everything we had and thrown it away."

He paused, turned to me and the tears started streaming down his face. "Richard, they are going to take our home."

His head dropped to his hands and the tears came faster and his breathing became more labored. "I just can't believe I could be so stupid. I really thought this would work. It was a great idea and if it had worked, it would have put us on easy street. How could I have been so stupid?"

His drawn face, the shaking of his hands, his inability to control his emotions told me I was dealing with a young man that was on the verge of a breakdown. The stress in his life had taken over his life, and he could no longer fight it. Slowly, but surely he was giving into it.

*Stress can wear you down and out.*

Reta wanted more than anything to be married and have children. At the age of 40 she felt her biological clock was ticking and there wasn't much time left to fulfill her dream. We talked about adoption, but she wanted to experience the thrill of childbirth.

She was a very successful business woman whose business had been her life for ten years. There really hadn't been any time for a relationship. The ones she had had all ended when the man couldn't handle her business drive. They would find her physically attractive, but mentally intimidating.

Then, one day she met Josh. His history was much like Reta's. They both came from dysfunctional families and connected through their pain. In several conversations I warned her about making pain the foundation for a relationship. She didn't want to hear it. Josh was the person for her.

Josh enjoyed what Reta did for him. He didn't have to do anything; she was there to take care of him. He didn't have to work; he didn't have to be responsible for his life. Reta was there to do it all for him.

During several conversations, Reta and I talked about the difference between having a healthy relationship and adopting someone in order to have someone in your life. She listened, but didn't want to hear what was being said. On more than one occasion she told me "Josh is the right person for me. I just know this is the right relationship."

Everything was going great until Reta got tired of taking care of Josh. He wouldn't do anything around the house. If he used dishes, they stayed dirty until Reta washed them. When he took his clothes off, he would just leave them where they fell. He didn't do anything but lie around and wait for Reta to come and take care of him. The day she had had enough was as she put it "the worst day of my life."

The day she confronted his behavior he went off on her. He emotionally pushed her and called her a "selfish bitch!" He couldn't understand how she could be so mean to him. In his words "you are worse than my mother ever was."

Reta fell apart. She called me, found out where I was and flew to see me. She was a mess when she arrived. Her eyes were swollen; her face was drawn and you could tell she arrived in emotional pieces.

As we sat at lunch and talked, she kept asking one question, "Why did I let him do this to me?"

I knew she wasn't looking for an answer from me. We had discussed this several times. What Josh was doing was not new; it was a pattern he had repeated since the relationship began. Things would get good; Josh would get scared and attack Reta. He would push her away and then, come back with a huge apology and a promise to not do it again.

She looked at me for a long moment and continued, "I know, I know. You and I have talked about this several times. I just don't know how to handle this."

I reached over, touched her arm and as she turned to me said, "There is only one question you need to focus on."

I paused long enough to get her attention. "You know what it is. Reta, is this relationship healthy for you? Does this relationship strengthen or weaken your life?"

There was this long look and then, the tears couldn't be contained. She looked away as she began to talk to me. "It sure isn't doing me any good. I give my best and just when I think it is going well, he attacks me emotionally. It is doing nothing but tearing my life apart."

"Then," I said with a sterner voice. "Is this relationship healthy for your life?"

"NO! It is making me less of a person. You told me sometime ago if it didn't add to my life, I needed to question whether it was right or not. I just wanted this to work."

*Stress plays no favorites. It doesn't care what you want; it will still attack your life.*

Alex wasn't looking for a job when the headhunter called him. He was content where he was. The company was good to him and for the first time he felt at home, BUT the headhunter presented him with an opportunity that sounded too good not to look at. They were willing to pay him 20% more than he was making and offer him a benefit package second to none. He jumped and it didn't take long to realize he had jumped into a frying pan.

He found me in the restaurant after I had finished my presentation. "I don't mean to interrupt you, but could I ask you a question?"

I looked up and could see the pain in his eyes. "Hey, sit down."

I didn't have to ask twice. He sat, looked at me for a moment and then said, "What do you do when you know you have made a huge mistake?"

"Depends," I said, "on what the mistake is."

"I have never been a real impulsive person until a few months ago. I had a great job, but reacted to what I thought was an opportunity. I looked and only saw the money. I should have slowed down and really examined the entire company. Now, five months into the job I have been informed they are closing my office, and I am going to be without a job."

There was a moment of silence as he emotionally slowed down. "I am so angry."

"Who are you angry at?"

"Everyone! I am angry at me for being so dumb. I am angry at the company for lying to me. I am angry at my old company for not talking me out of leaving. I have been so upset it has been physically affecting me. I went to my doctor this past week and he told me my blood pressure was really high. He wanted to know what was happening, and I unloaded on him. When I finished, he looked me squarely in the eye and told me to either handle my stress or it would handle me."

"You know he's right, don't you?"

"Yes! I guess I never understood how dangerous stress is to your life. I always knew it existed, but I never knew what it could do to you. This stuff can kill you!"

Alex is so right. This thing called stress can kill you! It is more than an emotional thing that can affect you; it is an enemy that can kill you. It really doesn't play favorites. It is present in every life, everyday and can do damage without you feeling its presence. Then, one day you awaken to what has happened to your life. For many it is too late.

Each year thousands of people die from stress related diseases. Talk to any health professional, and they will tell you the dangerous story of what stress can do to your life. They will talk to you about heart disease, about depression, about high blood pressure, about the mental, emotional and physical damage. They will repeat to you what Alex's doctor said to him. "Take care of your stress, or it will take care of you."

Here's the question: *How important is your life to you?* Is living important enough to take an honest look at your lifestyle? Are you willing to look at what might be attacking your life and stealing time from you?

When it comes to stress, too many are too cavalier about its place in their life. They joke about it; they avoid the situations that are causing it; they blame others and things for their life and in the process give negative stress a death grip on their life. Do you respect life? Do you enjoy living enough to stop avoiding and start facing those issues in your life that are mentally and emotionally taking a physical toll on your body?

John told me a few weeks after he had had open-heart surgery. "Richard, I went in for a simple physical and wound up in the operating room. My doctor told me I was the healthiest walking dead man he had ever seen."

There are so many John's out there. Every day they play a game of Russian Roulette with their life. They continually put more and more stress on their life by convincing their self they can handle it. They won't face what they are doing to their body. After all, they have plenty of life in front of them. I don't know who told them they were guaranteed tomorrow. Whoever did was lying to them. Stress can keep you from having the tomorrow you are working so hard today to achieve. What good is having lots of things, if you are dead? Stress is not a game! It is a fact. And the fact is, *it can kill you!*

**What Must You Do To Make Sure Stress Is Not Killing You?**

S    stay at a pace you can manage
T    take time for physicals
R    refuse to live reacting to events
E    enlist the help of others
S    sort through events, don't avoid them
S    seek to control stress, not eliminate

# DO YOU GET IT?

Ok, do you get it! Do you get the fact that when Stress is not controlled, it can kill you! That is more than a statement; it is a fact you can't afford to avoid. In this transitional world we are living in people's lives are being challenged on every front. With these challenges comes an increase in their personal stress.

When this happens, you have options. You can run from the stress and increase it, or you can slow down and face the stress and take away its ability to do damage to you. It is your choice!

Ralph was one of my Private Coaching students. When he came to talk about us working together, this is what he said, "Richard, I am so tired of running. All I do everyday is get up and race through this thing I call a life. The reality is, it is not a life. It is simply me existing by not facing anything. I have become a master at avoiding things. I have finally realized I am killing myself by doing that. I have to stop! I keep telling myself what I have to do, but always have a reason why this is not the right time."

"Ralph, I agree with you, but are you ready to honestly face your life with the honesty this is going to require, look at what needs to be done, be strong enough to implement the needed improvements and do it consistently?"

"I have to! If I don't this stress is going to kill me."

"You didn't listen to what I asked you! It is not about *having to*. It is about being willing to do it. There is a difference between *having to do* something and *being willing to do it*. Now, are you willing to consistently do the things you are going to have to do to get your stress under control?"

"Richard, you don't know the stress I am feeling as
I hear you ask me that question. I have been at this junction
before, and said I have to do this, started and reverted back to
where I felt safe. What a joke! I was kidding myself."

He paused, took a deep breath and said with a voice
of conviction, "YES! I am willing to commit to doing with
consistency what I know I need to do."

I wish you could meet Ralph today. He is calmer, paced
and living, rather than existing in what was his stressful world.

Controlling stress is more than a thought; it is a lifestyle
change. It is you being honest with yourself, realizing too many
times you are rhetoric, rather than action. The result of you
being chatter without action is just more stress.

How does this negative stress kill you? *First, it
constantly nibbles at your spirit.* It challenges you with doubt,
with fear, with anger, with depression and an entire family of
negative emotions it brings to your existence. Over a period
of time, it wears your spirit down and replaces it with an
increasing anxiety you just can't get rid of.

How does this negative stress kill you? *It increases
your confusion about your life.* The more confused you are
about your life, the more challenging it becomes to take
positive action. What does this confusion do? It causes you to
play the "what if" game. That is such a dangerous game. Why?
You can't answer a "what if" question! "What if" is all about
you doubting yourself. What does doubt do? It erodes your self
trust and leaves you second guessing any and every decision
you make. That will push your stress level to a dangerous level.
Confusion is a thief that is capable of stealing life from you.

How does this negative stress kill you? *It lessens your
inner resolve to seek improvement.* Do you have any idea how

many times I have heard, "I give up! There is nothing else I can do. This is just the way it is going to be, so why try any more."

That is simply giving the situation control of your life, rather than you seeking the understanding for you to have control. When you give up, you shut your imagination down and turn your emotions up. The result is negative stress having free reign of your life.

How does this negative stress kill you? *It leaves you staring at yesterday, rather than standing in today preparing for tomorrow.* There is no life in yesterday; just a library of events for you to draw from. Those events are either filled with lessons to build on or reasons why you can't.

When you are standing in today preparing for tomorrow, you seek the lessons from yesterday's events and apply them through behavior to improve your life.

When you are staring at yesterday, you look for the reasons why your life isn't happening the way you wanted it to.

The difference between these two is whether you are growing and building a better life for yourself, or whether you are staring at the perceived wrongs and justifying, through your reasons and excuses, why you are a prisoner in your own body.

Your life is YOUR choice! As much as many don't like to accept that, it is a fact. You make choices and with the choices comes a pathway to walk. Stress comes into play with each decision you make. When you make decisions that will improve your life, there is an element of stress. But, this stress is healthy stress. It calms you down and gives you the foundation of belief that keeps you moving forward at a controlled pace. The moments of uncertainty you will feel are controlled by your inner belief this is right for your life and the self trust that knows you can do it!

When you work against what you know you should be doing, the result is negative stress. This stress will attack you and keep you at war with yourself. This is a war you can't win! The main weapons negative stress uses against you are fear, doubt, worrying and the feeling that none of this is going to work.

Stress is a fact! What you do with the stress your life will have is YOUR choice! As we have talked about in the pages of this book, there is always the opportunity to *control the stress in your life.* It will take an awareness of where you are in your life and the willingness to take positive action. How do you build an inner foundation that provides you with the strength to keep your stress on the positive side? Let me suggest some Building Blocks For Controlling The Stress In Your Life. They are not magical, but will provide you with some tips to always come back to and review.

1.  Always monitor the pace of your life and be certain you are in control of your life, and it is not in control of you.

2.  Know your tolerance level and don't push yourself beyond it.

3.  Don't let emotional issues build up in your life. Confront anything or anyone who is attacking you emotionally.

4.  Don't invest energy in the things you can't control. They will distract you.

5.  Surround your life with people who support your dream; remove those who are there to criticize what you want for your life. They don't care about you anyway!

6. Do your research before you step into the adventure. The more facts you are armed with, the less stress there is in making the decision.

7. Be clear on what you want to achieve before you start the journey.

8. Understand the fears you are going to face and confront them upfront.

9. Look for the lesson in every event your life is handed and keep a journal of those lessons. The journal will become your reference guide for decisions.

10. Before you say "yes" to anything in your life, pause and ask this question, "Will this feed my confusion or strengthen my clarity?" Make this the foundational question for making decisions in your life.

Remember, *it is not about eliminating the stress from your life; it is about controlling the stress.* The more you seek to eliminate your stress, the greater the stress will become. Slow down, take that deep breath and see what you need to do to control your stress and do it! You will turn an enemy that can kill you into a friend that supports you.

# NOTES

# NOTES

# NOTES

## ABOUT THE AUTHOR

**Richard Flint** is one of those unique people who has been given the ability to see the clarity in the midst of what looks confusing. Since 1980, he has been sharing his insights and philosophies with audiences all over North America. He is known as the person who knows you even though he has never met you. He has written 14 books, recorded over 50 audio albums/cds, and filmed 27 videos. Beyond being an author, he is a nationally recognized speaker, a lifestyle coach to many who are seeking to stop repeating and start achieving, and a frequent guest on radio and television talk shows. But more than all this, you will find him to be a friend whose understandings can calm your emotional confusion.

## SERVICES AVAILABLE

On-site training, consulting and keynote speaking. *It's simple.* Richard Flint can make your people better. He can customize any of his programs and come right to your company's door. He also provides a full range of in-house consulting services, and is always delighted to add sparkle to your next corporate or association meeting with a stimulating keynote presentation designed just for you.

For more information about Richard's on-site services, call our Marketing Department at 1-800-368-8255.

Whether you have 30 or 3,000 people to make better, Richard Flint is the answer.

## Share It With Others

To order copies of this book,
Call 1-800-368-8255
or (757) 873-7722
or visit
www.RichardFlint.com

Special quantity discounts are available
for bulk purchases.

Please allow 2-3 weeks for US delivery.
Canada & International orders
please allow 4-6 weeks for delivery.

Other Books by Richard Flint, CSP:

I Need A Life!

Behavior Never Lies

The Truth About Stress

Breaking Free

Building Blocks *For Strengthening Your Life*

Building Blocks *For Strengthening Your Relationships*

Building Blocks *For Improving Customer Relationships*

Building Blocks *For Controlling Stress*